W9-BZH-990

REDWOOD

WITHDRAWN

LIBRARY
NEWPORT
R.I.

GARDNER BLANCHARD PERRY FUND

OF CARRIAGES AND KINGS

OF
CARRIAGES
AND
KINGS

BY

Frederick John Gorst

WITH

Beth Andrews

THOMAS Y. CROWELL COMPANY

NEW YORK

Copyright © 1956 by Frederick John Gorst and Beth Andrews

All rights reserved. No part of this book may be
reproduced in any form, except by a reviewer,
without the permission of the publisher.

Manufactured in the United States of America

Library of Congress Catalog Card No. 56-7231

6
.G6874A

For
ABBY and AGNES

Grateful acknowledgement is made to
Dr. A. P. Merrill and Mrs. George H. Taylor
for their many courtesies, and to
Clark Andrews, who gave so generously
of his time and advice during
the preparation of this manuscript.

Contents

GLOSSARY OF TERMS USED BY SERVANTS

"The Old Man" .... Steward

"Flunkies" or "Shiny-Tails" ..... Footmen, because of the silver and brass buttons worn on their tail-coats.

"Buttons" and rarely "Footboy" .. Page Boy

"Silk and Keys" .... Housekeeper, because of her rustling silk dress and jingling keys which announced her approach like a bell.

"Gentleman's Gentleman" .... Valet

"Frenchy" .... Chef

"Odd Men" .... Housemen

"Tigers" .... Small grooms

"Strappers" .... Stablemen

"Biddies" or "Pot Wallopers" .... Kitchen maids
  or "Pearl Divers"

"The Lead" .... First footman

"The Follow Up" .... Second or assisting
                                   footman

"Slops" .... Housemaids

"Grub" .... All food

"The Box" .... Driver's seat on a car-
                                   riage

"Gillie" .... An outdoor male serv-
                                   ant in Scotland who
                                   attends to the hunting
                                   and shooting.

"Still Room" .... A room connected with
                                   the kitchen where cof-
                                   fee, tea, or the like are
                                   made and the finer ar-
                                   ticles for the table are
                                   prepared and stored.

"Trifle" .... A dessert made of
                                   spongecake and maca-
                                   roons soaked in wine
                                   or liqueur, with jam,
                                   whipped cream, and
                                   any kind of fruit de-
                                   sired.

OF CARRIAGES AND KINGS

1

My Youth

I AM now almost seventy-five years old, and one of my greatest pleasures is to relive the bright shining days of my youth. And it is fortunate that I am able to recall the past with a clarity and vividness that is not given to every man in the "outpost of advancing day." Perhaps it is easier for me to recollect my younger years because my memories are so full of colorful pictures of grandeur, of festive elegance, and gaiety. Indeed, I think of those exciting and wonderful years almost every day of my life, and I remember them better than most things which happened yesterday.

More than half a century has elapsed as I now part the curtain upon the scenes of pomp and circumstance in which I lived: a world of Kings and Queens, Dukes and Duchesses, Lords and Ladies. I lived and served in the golden Edwardian era of pageantry and magnificence—I was a Royal footman.

To be in the Royal service was the hope and ambition of

every servant in England; it was the top rung of the ladder! But the ascent to the summit was painstakingly slow, often discouraging. Sometimes there was heartache—and you needed a full share of luck. In my profession, as in many others, it was necessary to serve a long and exacting apprenticeship in order to achieve "faultless perfection" in the performance of innumerable duties. For example, when I was a little page boy, I had to learn to carry a heavy pitcher of hot milk every evening through the dark, winding corridors of St. Aiden's Theological College to the Reverend Beibetz, without spilling a drop.

One night, the Reverend, observing my distress, which was ill-concealed beneath my rosy cheeks, said with a twinkle in his eye,

"Frederick, now you are bringing hot milk to a tired, old man. But someday, if you work very hard, who knows —you may even serve Royalty!"

Years later when I indeed waited upon His Majesty, King Edward VII, and deftly handed him a golden platter of Egyptian quail at a regal banquet, I realized that the kindly words of the Reverend Beibetz had been touched by prophecy. But how long it had all taken to come true! And how long ago it all began!

I was born in Liverpool on November 13, 1881, while Victoria was still our great, good Queen. I was the ninth child of my parents, Henry and Mary Ann Gorst, who named me Frederick after the Emperor of Germany, and John for my father's brother. As the children were born, my father gave some of them Biblical or historical names: William Luke, Henry James, Lillian Elizabeth, Margaret

Ann, and Albert Edward. . . . He must have found it increasingly difficult to find enough euphonious names to go around, because, as time went on, there were thirteen of us in all.

I was literally one of a baker's dozen, for that was my father's profession. In addition to his bakery business, he sold provender to the large dairies in Liverpool which kept their herds in adjacent barns. When Mother took us to Liverpool, it was not unusual to see the cows going for an airing in the streets, somehow reminiscent of the sacred cows of India. We felt sorry for these poor animals who were living their lives so unnaturally, coming from the country to be stabled in the city.

My mother was an extraordinary woman. She worked six hours every day in my father's bakery. She designed and supervised the making of all of the wedding cakes. Like an artist, she was constantly creating new recipes and experimenting with new combinations of candied fruits and spices. There was hardly a wedding in Liverpool that was not graced by one of Mother's cakes.

We lived in a comfortable old house, high on a hill, in Everton, overlooking the city. When we were not in school, we spent most of our time doing our assigned household tasks. My mother was deeply religious and thoroughly disciplined, and she applied her own vigorous standards to her children. We helped with the supper every night until the last dish was neatly put away. Then Mama saw to it that we did our homework, and that thirteen pairs of hands polished thirteen pairs of shoes. We were thirteen youngsters who learned from my mother's example that life would make demands on us and that we had to be helpful and self-reliant.

Every Saturday morning it was my task to scrub the lobby, steps, and the sidewalk in front of our house. This may have been the era of the combustion engine, but it was still the era of the hand scrubbing brush! When I finished this job, I "raddled" the window sills. I cleaned the sills and applied the "Red Raddle Powder." Back and forth—polishing away, hour after hour. The shiny, red sills set off the red geraniums and magenta fuchsias which bloomed all summer long in the window boxes. And because it was my handiwork, I thought our house was the neatest and prettiest on the hill.

My eldest sister, Lily, bright-eyed and gangling at thirteen, supervised the younger girls who cleaned inside the house, the kitchen, and scullery. When supper was served in the kitchen on Saturday night, the brass fenders and oven doors shone like mirrors. All of the cooking was done in the large, open fireplace and the room was cosy and warm. On one side of the fireplace was the built-in oven, and on the other was a hot water heater which functioned overtime on Saturday nights.

This was the busiest and merriest evening of the week: it was bath night. A large, tin tub with shaped sides was placed in the center of the floor. The three eldest children, Will, Meg, and Lily, took charge and bathed their ten younger brothers and sisters, one by one. If you figure conservatively ten gallons of water to a bath, then some one hundred and thirty gallons of hot water accomplished this miracle of purification. This was the time my father thought most appropriate to read from the Bible, which he did in a deep and solemn voice.

Though sometimes I fell asleep while Papa was reading, I was always his favorite son. Wherever he went, he invariably took me with him, and this put the other children's noses a bit out of joint. Sometimes my mother dressed me in a Little Lord Fauntleroy suit which I hated because I thought it made me look like a girl. But my father often came to the rescue and restored my pride. When I went fishing with him, I wore the clothes of a real fisherman.

On Sundays, during the summer, he arose at six. I was happy as a skylark when he awakened me on these exciting mornings. We went down to the landing stage in a tiny cove, not far from the spot where the Mersey River ran into the Irish Sea.

My father kept his fishing smack moored there during the week, and an old fellow, Isaac Crosby, tended it for him. I loved the old man because I always associated him with a feeling of freedom and adventure when he turned the sheets to the wind. Then as the "Polly" moved away from her mooring, Crosby went back to the dock in his dinghy. Each time we sailed down the river, we waved to each other until our boat was out of sight and we had almost reached the open sea, pointed toward the fishing grounds.

At times, the Irish Sea can become squally without warning. Then my father would put me into the cockpit with the ropes and tackle, so that I wouldn't be washed overboard. But my father was a good sailor and always made it back to the landing stage—no matter how hard it blew.

Every Sunday evening at eight o'clock, without fail,

fifteen members of the Gorst family entered St. Chad's Episcopal Church, thus assuring the Reverend Mosedale of, at least, a modest congregation for the evensong, the Anglican vesper service. I loved music and I listened very attentively to the beautiful soprano voices of the boys' choir. How I always wished to be one of them! I practiced for a long time before I was able to sing the hymns and then I became a substitute choir boy. My voice improved as I grew, so fairly soon I was made a regular member of the choir, and the Reverend Mosedale chose me for special coaching. When I was twelve, I became the soloist of the boys' choir and no little chorister ever piped more devoutly.

As I look back to those years, I suppose I was as contented as most children in my circumstances. I was progressing nicely in school, I had hopes of becoming a singer and a musician, and I felt secure in the love of my parents, and my brothers and sisters.

But one evening at tea time, my father came home and sat down in the armchair in the kitchen. He looked tired and ill, and somehow very old. He stared blankly into the fireplace for a long time before he finally spoke.

"Polly," he said quietly to my mother, "I have something terrible to tell you. I have lost the provender business and we are ruined. We will have nothing left when the bankruptcy is declared."

We waited in shocked silence for my mother to answer. What would Mama say? What would we do? After a few moments, she slowly raised her head and looked at all of us. Then she turned to Papa and said almost in a whisper,

"Henry, if that is the way the good Lord has decreed

it must be, then we will accept it. We will manage somehow, and all of us will help."

Everything we had was taken away and we moved to a
house farther up the hill, which we rented for one pound
a month. What little furniture was left, we carried up to
the new house ourselves. Even though we were now poor,
to my youthful eyes, the only difference was that I shared
a room with three of my brothers instead of one. Soon
afterward my eldest brother was apprenticed as a printer's
devil, and I began to feel that I must also do my part. So,
at the age of twelve, I set out to find my first job.

After roving the streets for two weeks, I found a position
with the *Financial Times* of Liverpool. I sat on a high stool
in an open window and sold the papers, straight from the
presses, to the passersby. From my work, which began at
eight and ended at six, I earned five shillings a week.

After seven months with the *Times*, I heard of a better
position from a boy who sold papers with me, and we
resigned together to become counterboys at the British
Workman's Public House. Though the work began at five,
three hours earlier, and ended at six, I made but six shillings
a week. Even so, that extra shilling seemed like a large
increase.

It allowed me to indulge a taste for tea and cakes. Once
a week I went to the Liverpool Station Restaurant and sat
at the counter. I ordered a cup of tea, a crumpet, and a
piece of "light cake." I squandered a sixpence, so I added
the remaining one to my savings.

However, as the months went by, I found it more and
more difficult to get up at four every morning. I felt
perpetually tired and weary, but I didn't want Mama to

know, because I had been able to give her five shillings a
week.

One evening after work, when I went to choir practice
at St. Chad's, the Reverend Mosedale stopped me in the
corridor.

"Freddy, are you quite sure you're feeling well?" he
asked. "It seems to me that you look rather thin, my boy.
Let's go into my study and have a little chat."

As I followed him into the large, pleasant room, I felt
miserable and unhappy.

"Now, Freddy," the Reverend said, "suppose you sit
down and tell me all about it."

He spoke so benignly that I could no longer hold back
the tears, and in short, disjointed sentences I tried to explain
that my job at the Public House was more than I could
bear. The Reverend listened patiently to my troubles, then
gave me his handkerchief, patted my head, and put a
comforting arm around my shoulder.

"Freddy," he said after a moment's thought, "I believe
I can get you a job that you will like. I will write a letter
to my friend, the Reverend Joseph Beibetz, and ask him if
you can go to St. Aiden's as a page boy. That is the theological college which I once attended, and I dare say you
will be happier there. You can learn a great many things
and you can improve yourself by emulating the good
people you will serve. Best of all, you will be learning a
valuable trade and you should be able to help your mother.
I can't promise, of course, but I will try."

I left the Reverend Mosedale's study and ran all the way
up the hill to tell Mama. She shook her head, saying only

that she thought St. Aiden's was quite far from Liverpool and that I was much too young to go away from home.

Like any young boy with a fixed purpose, I would not accept my mother's opinion. I pleaded doggedly with her to let me go. It was the first thing I mentioned in the morning and the last thing at night. Finally, either because I exhausted her or because she saw some wisdom in my logic, she reluctantly consented. And when the Reverend Mosedale came late one afternoon to confirm the fact that a good job was open for me at St. Aiden's, Mama actually seemed satisfied that everything was all right.

"Don't worry, my dear Mrs. Gorst," Reverend Mosedale said sympathetically, "Freddy will be in good hands. I dare say he will miss you for a while, but he will have more paternal care at the college than he will know what to do with!"

My mother's last resistance disappeared in a smile of acceptance.

The last week at home was spent in preparation for my leave-taking. Lily mended and brushed my Sunday suit, and my two white shirts and linens were clean and tidy. I took a tintype of my parents, my hymnal, and an album of mottos and pressed flowers which Davey Driscoll, my best friend, gave me when I said good-bye to him.

I was sorry to leave him because he had grown so frail. I feared I might not see him again because they said he was developing the lung sickness, as tuberculosis was then called. I promised Davey that I would write to him once a week and describe everything I saw and learned. But for now, all I knew was that I was to have a page boy's livery and ten pounds a year. I could hardly wait to begin.

The day finally came for me to leave, August 10, 1894. Mama took me on the tram to the Birkenhead Ferry Landing. She bent down to kiss me and whispered, "Be brave and do your best."

As I watched Mama walk away from me, I realized that I was alone for the first time in my life. For an instant I wanted to run after her, but instead I carried my battered, tin trunk on to the deck and ran to the bow of the ship. In a moment the bells signaled and the landing gates closed. And as the ferry began to glide slowly across the Mersey River, my fear and indecision gradually ebbed away. Then as I looked at the opposite shore, a surge of excitement suddenly came over me. There, not very far away, was the beginning of my new life.

A Page at St. Aiden's

As the swaying trolley stopped in Claughton, I jumped down and put my trunk on my shoulder, ready to walk up the hill to St. Aiden's Theological College. Only the towers were visible on the crest and it loomed like a fairy castle in the morning mist. A weather vane on the turret moved in the soft wind and the low, hanging clouds moved lightly across the sky. My trunk seemed to grow heavier as I walked up the road, and my Eton collar grew tighter as I neared the imposing building. I wondered if my knickerbockers were still properly creased, and if anybody could tell that the knee socks I was wearing belonged to my sister.

I walked up the broad flight of steps to the front door and lifted the large, wrought iron knocker which resounded so loudly as it struck that a flock of rooks rose out of the oak trees like a shimmering black cloud. The door was quickly opened by a tall man with silvery hair and a red face, dressed in a black livery.

"And who are you, I'd like to know?" he said.

"I'm Freddy Gorst, the new page boy."

"Well, well, now fancy that! And you'd better be getting around to the back door where you belong. That's where you're supposed to come in!"

I had been at St. Aiden's less than five minutes and I had already made my first mistake. As I walked around the curving driveway to the rear courtyard, a small lady came toward me. She wore a black dress with a tiny lace collar, and the largest bunch of keys I had ever seen were jangling from her waist.

"Good morning, young man," she said. "I am sure you are the new page. I am Miss Giles, the housekeeper, and I'm pleased to meet you."

"I'm Freddy," I said somewhat shyly, "I'm very happy to see you, Miss Giles. I do hope I'm what you expected."

"I think so," she said as she looked me up and down. "But now I'll take you up to the third floor and show you your room. I've tried to make it a bit homey for you. There're muslin curtains on the window and an easy chair by the fireplace."

"That's very kind of you," I said. As I walked along beside Miss Giles, I thought how wonderful it would be to have a room with a fireplace all to myself, and not be obliged to share it with anyone, not even my brother. When we reached the third floor, Miss Giles led the way to a room in the far corner.

"This is your room," she said. "I do hope you'll be comfortable. And here's a wee scarf I made for your dresser. Now you can unpack and arrange your things."

As soon as Miss Giles left, I put the scarf on the dresser.

I noticed that she had embroidered a bouquet of violets in the center. If it had been made of the rarest velvet, I could not have cherished it more. I stood my parents' picture on the mantle, and placed my linens in the drawers. I thought the cupboard would be the place to hang up my Sunday suit and store my trunk, so I opened the door.

As it swung back, I saw my page boy livery: a dark red jacket, with a brighter red collar and white taping, carefully buttoned over the long, dark blue trousers. There were eight shiny brass buttons on the coat. I could not resist putting the suit on immediately. But I had only stepped into the trousers when there was a knock on the door.

The tall man in the black livery who had first greeted me entered. As I looked up at him, he seemed to tower over me like a giant.

"I am Mr. Taylor, the butler," he said, peering down at me. "I notice you have found your livery and I see that it fits you—at least the pants do. It fit the last boy, too, but the last boy didn't fit *it!* You are to wear it only when you wait at table, and when you are on duty. And one more thing, mind you, don't go to bed and sleep in it! Now, dress yourself quickly and come down to the kitchen."

I put on my livery and looked at myself in the small mirror over the dresser which, unfortunately, only reproduced my reflection from the neck up. So I took it off the wall and started at my collar, moving it slowly down to the tops of my shoes. Although I was only able to see myself in fractions, I felt that the composite picture must be a very satisfactory one. I was delighted with the fit of the shoulders, and the way the jacket buttoned up to my neck. I was ready to work.

As I went down three steep flights of steps and through a maze of corridors, some of the students were standing in the downstairs hall. I asked them how to find the kitchen. And even though I was in a great hurry, I thought that they were looking at me approvingly. Surely it was my new livery. . . .

Finally, I found the pantry. Mr. Taylor was taking down the loaves of freshly baked bread from the huge copper trays which were stacked as high as his head. He was slicing them expertly on a cutting board, but when he saw me he stopped and abruptly sat down on a small green stool. I thought he looked like a bullfrog on a lily pad.

"Freddy," he said, "we serve dinner at 12:30 promptly. Your first task is to fill each one of these fifteen toast dishes. Make the toast in the open oven, and put the top on each dish to keep it hot. Watch it carefully and be mindful not to burn it. Then come into the kitchen and I will teach you how to hand the maids the vegetable dishes from the serving trays."

I thought this was a very short lesson indeed, but I soon found myself in the enormous dining hall helping to serve dinner to seventy-five students and the faculty. Although I was uneasy, and felt that at any moment I might drop a plate, every dish of potatoes and boiled cabbage safely reached its destination.

Then, after dinner was served and I had eaten mine on a small shelf in the pantry, I helped the cook and the maids with the cleaning up in the scullery. It took only three-quarters of an hour to serve the dinner, but it took almost three hours to put things in order afterward.

Then I was instructed in tallying the coal chart by Mr. Taylor. Each student had an open fireplace in his room, and when he wished to have a scuttle of coal brought up, he left a notice slip in the "coal box" which hung on the wall outside the dining room. It was necessary for me to mark down the deliveries opposite each student's name on the coal chart, as there was an extra charge for coal. I also learned that I was responsible for carrying about forty scuttles to the rooms each day and seeing that every order was filled.

"You know, Freddy, it's the only heat we have," Mr. Taylor said. "So you've got an important job, especially in the winter, when it gets jolly cold around here."

After supper was served, Miss Giles told me to walk to Claughton to fetch the evening mail at the village post office, and as soon as I returned, to take a tray with a pitcher of hot milk, which she always prepared herself, to the Vice-Principal, the Reverend Beibetz. Miss Giles said that this errand, which was to be done every evening sharply at nine o'clock, would conclude my duties for the day. "Keep a steady hand," she cautioned, "the pitcher is heavy."

I carried the tray, which Miss Giles handed me, carefully through the dark halls to the Reverend Beibetz's study in the front corridor. I was very pleased that my hand was steady and that I didn't spill a single drop. When I knocked and entered, he said:

"Good evening, Freddy. Miss Giles told me that you had arrived and that she was very pleased with you. I expected as much because my colleague, the Reverend Mosedale, gave you an excellent recommendation. Every evening when you bring my hot milk, you may say your prayers with me. In this way, I will be able to see you every day and I will know how you are getting on. And I think it's just time for prayers right now."

When prayers were over and I had thanked the Reverend Beibetz for giving me the chance to work at St. Aiden's, I walked back to my room through the long deserted corridors. I thought of my parents and all my sisters and brothers. This was such a big place and there were so many strange faces here. It would take a long time for me to make any friends—except possibly Miss Giles, who was waiting for me now at the door of my room.

"I came to say good night to you, Freddy," she said pleasantly. "I have been here for twenty-four years and you have been here only one day. Anytime you feel like it—just come down to my sitting room for a chat. I suggest that you go to bed now. Tomorrow is another day and there will be more to learn. And by the way, a storm is coming so keep your windows closed. Sleep well and pleasant dreams!"

I had no sooner crawled under the covers than there was a loud roll of thunder, and the rain began to beat against the windows. I sat up in bed thinking about my first day at St. Aiden's. I felt almost too tired to sleep, but I must have dozed off. I awoke with a start, remembering a dream in which I had been counting loaves of bread which were all as tall as Mr. Taylor. The room seemed stuffy, so I opened the window to see if it was still raining.

The storm had stopped, and the stars were bright in the

sky. Through the clear night air I heard the chirping of crickets and the sound of a dog barking far off in the distance. I didn't sleep any more that night.

The next day was beautiful and warm. The linnets were singing their early morning song as I walked to Claughton to fetch the morning mail. While I was in the village store, which was also the post office, I saw a bicycle leaning against a rack of garden tools.

"Is it for sale?" I asked the man behind the counter.

"Do you want to buy it for yourself?" he said, "because if you do, you can have it for five shillings."

That was quite a sum for me to take out of my small savings, but thinking of coasting down the hill every day, I decided it was worth while.

"I'll reserve it," I replied, "and I'll bring you the money tonight when I call for the evening mail. I am the new page boy at St. Aiden's."

"Well," he answered pleasantly, "I think, in that case, you can take it right along with you."

Proudly I pushed my new bicycle up the hill, and then I realized that I now had something else to learn. I had to learn to ride it! But that would not be too difficult, because I was to have several hours to myself in the afternoon. When I returned, I asked Mr. Taylor where I could practice riding my bicycle.

"I think the basement will do nicely," he said. "It's almost big enough to run the Derby. But for now, Freddy, I think you had better keep your mind on your work! Go down to the boot room and help Charles, the houseman."

I found him in a room in the basement with seventy-five pairs of shoes on two long shelves arranged according to the students' room numbers. By noon I had heard the story of Charles' life, and all the shoes had been well polished and returned to their owners.

After dinner when the chores were done, I ran to the basement, and within the short space of an hour, I could balance quite well, riding from one end of the huge cavern to the other. As I gained confidence in myself, I thought how proud Mama would be if she knew that I could ride a bicycle. I would write to her and Davey Driscoll and tell them both about everything that had already happened. Not only did I have a page boy livery but I owned a bicycle as well!

Being able to ride around the countryside enlarged my small world. I followed the lanes over the rolling hills, look-ing at the hedgerows, and the stone fences between the verdant meadows, and the rose-covered cottages with their lovely little flower gardens that gave the landscape such a friendly air. It was all so old and the sleepy villages looked as though they had not changed in hundreds of years. I began to know some of the people who lived in the thatched-roof cottages in Claughton and when I made my trips to fetch the mail, they would often call from the doorways:

"Hey, Freddy, how goes it? Would you like a cup of tea?"

When I had time I went in and joined them. I loved their simple cottages and the tidy kitchens where they had their tea. The stone floors had been trodden upon for centuries and scrubbed almost as white as marble.

My fondness for cycling did, however, get me into a bit of a mess with the Reverend Beibetz. He had a very

fine Rudge-Whiteworth machine in which he took a great
deal of pride. He arranged with me to keep it clean, and in
return I was allowed to ride it occasionally when he wasn't
using it.

One beautiful afternoon I got the wanderlust. Although
I had been at St. Aiden's for almost a year, I had never
explored the roads beyond Claughton. So I took the Rudge-
Whiteworth, rather than my own bicycle, and went for a
long ride. I completely forgot myself and the time—I almost forgot that I had to go back to St. Aiden's. When I
returned, Mr. Taylor met me at the back door and led me
into the pantry by the ear. He glowered at me and shook
me.

"You young rascal!" he said. "You might like to know
that the Reverend Beibetz had a christening in Bidestone
and had to borrow someone else's machine! It may also
interest you to hear that he was as mad as a hornet, and
something tells me you'll find out about this from the old
boy himself!"

When I brought the Reverend Beibetz his hot milk precisely at nine o'clock, I was quaking and too afraid to say
"good evening."

After his usual greeting, there were no prayers. Instead,
there was a lecture. He began by referring to Chapter Six,
Verse Thirty-one of St. Luke:

"And as ye would that men should do to you,
    do ye also to them likewise."

When he finished, I told him that I had failed to notice
the time while I was enjoying myself on his bicycle but
that I had not meant to cause him trouble.

He looked at me over the rims of his glasses and said,

"There is another text from St. Luke, also from Chapter Eleven, Verse Four:

" 'And forgive us our sins,

For we also forgive everyone that is indebted to us.' "

Then he said, "Freddy, now we will say our prayers."

After the last "amen," I said, "Thank you, sir, for your forgiveness and your kindness. I will never take your bicycle again without your permission."

I was constantly learning something new about my job. Step by step, Mr. Taylor taught me how to serve at table, how to hand the platters, the correct way to remove the plates, and finally, the actual setting of the table itself. He also drilled me in "backing up" the butler or maid whom I was assisting.

"When you know this, you'll have mastered the groundwork of our trade, Freddy," he said. "It may take another six months but you must learn it, if you ever want to become a footman. When the roast is served, you back up, or follow up, the maid right away with the gravy, or when the fish is served, you're johnny-on-the-spot with the sauce. One more important thing—see that the dishes come to the table piping hot."

"But, Mr. Taylor," I asked, "how do we manage it when the kitchen is so far from the dining room?"

"By hustling, Freddy, that's how you do it, and that's why we keep the serving dishes covered. In some establishments where the kitchen is in the basement and the dining room is on the ground floor, they use hot bricks and alcohol stoves with trivets, but we haven't the staff for that.

"However, you're learning, Freddy, and I think you already know enough to try your hand. I have an important test coming up for you. You are to help at the Principal's house on Sunday night when the Rev. Harding and Mrs. Harding give their customary supper for twelve students. You are to assist the cook in the kitchen and back up Jane, the parlormaid."

"I would love to back up Jane, the parlor maid," I said.

Sunday afternoon, after I attended the service in the chapel, I went to the residence of the Principal, the Reverend E. Elmer Harding, which was not very far from the main building.

Jane greeted me cheerfully: "Hello, Buttons, I've been expecting you."

She was the prettiest and youngest maid at St. Aiden's. Her uniform rustled as she moved about the kitchen, and over it she wore a long, starched apron with scalloped suspenders and a bodice. A fancy, puffed cap of lace hid most of her light brown curls.

Her first order to me was to take fourteen dinner plates, for the main course, from the kitchen up to the dining room. I went up the dark, narrow steps and as I turned to enter the room, I slipped on the highly waxed floor. As I fell, all of the plates flew out of my hands. Some hit the thick carpet with a sickening thud and others rolled like white hoops to the walls. I picked myself up, shaking and trembling. But when I looked down at the scene of carnage, it wasn't as bad as I expected. Not a single plate was broken! What a stroke of luck! Some guardian angel must have been hovering near me. But so was Mrs. Harding!

She came into the room like a ruffled hen and seemed to cackle as she said:

"You stupid, clumsy, oafish boy!"

Picking up the plates and piling them on the sideboard, I answered meekly:

"Oh, Mrs. Harding, I'm so sorry, I didn't mean to do it, please excuse me. . . ."

But she paid no attention and continued:

"Do you think those plates are clean after having been on the floor? Take every last one of them down and wash them again. Don't you dare to put them back on the table!"

I wondered how all the plates could be soiled, but I didn't want to say anything more to Mrs. Harding. I finished stacking them and I carefully made two trips, carrying seven each time, and safely delivered them all to the scullery sink. I was crying when I got there.

"What's the matter, Freddy?" Jane asked. "Those plates were washed just before I sent you up with them."

I told her what had happened but Jane only seemed to be amused. She laughed and said, "We all know her well, she's really ever so nice. She barks much worse than she bites. So, dry your eyes—you're spoiling your nice page-boy suit with your salty tears."

Even though the rest of the dinner went smoothly and I made no more mistakes, I could hardly wait to get back to the college. I wanted to see Miss Giles. When I returned, I found her in her sitting room working on her accounts.

"Is anything wrong?" she asked quietly.

"Yes," I said. And I described the tragedy in all its detail. I told her that Mrs. Harding couldn't have hurt me more if she had slapped my face, and that no one could ever make me go there again.

Miss Giles listened patiently until I had finished. Then

she said, "I will explain to Mrs. Harding how conscientious you have been about your work since the first day you came over a year ago, and I am sure that she will be more patient the next time you go there. However, since this incident has come up, I think you should understand its real meaning. Sometimes when you are in service, Freddy, the gentry will do things that seem quite unreasonable and unjust, and you will find it very hard not to be able to stand up for your rights. Instead, learn to stand on your dignity. You'll get along much better that way."

In the course of many months I did get along much better, but there were several occasions when I stood on my dignity rather unsteadily.

St. Aiden's was honored by a visit from a noted member of the Church of England, the Lord Bishop of North Queensland. Before he arrived there had been a good deal of preparation and instruction. I was given the duty of awakening His Lordship every morning at seven forty-five, and at the same time, I was to deliver his shaving water.

Mr. Taylor coached me and told me exactly how it was to be done.

"Freddy," he said, "carry the pitcher of hot water carefully up to the Lord Bishop's room on a tray, knock gently on the door until he answers. When he asks who is there, you say, 'Your shaving water, my Lord.' And then you enter and put it down on the washstand. Is that understood?"

"Yes, Mr. Taylor, I understand perfectly," I said.

The next morning at seven forty-one, I left the pantry with a pitcher of boiling hot water on a tray which Mr.

Taylor handed me. I made my way slowly through the corridors to the Bishop's rooms and knocked.

"Who is there?" he asked in a resonant, bass voice.

"The Lord's shaving water, sir," I replied.

"The Lord is not here," answered the Bishop, "but I would very much like to use it myself."

I came in very flustered and put down the water on the washstand. As I started to leave, the Bishop said,

"Thank you for this most unusual ablution, and I believe that one good turn deserves another." Then he handed me a brand-new shilling which I added to my savings in my little tin trunk.

Since I had been at St. Aiden's I had managed to accumulate over £20. The students had given me tips at the end of the terms and I had never spent any of my salary. When I went home for the first time, I was able to give my mother £20, and I still remember how pleased she was. She said, with tears in her eyes, "Freddy, you are probably the richest young man in Liverpool."

It was a wonderful week that I spent with my family. But one dark event overshadowed my homecoming. My childhood friend, Davey Driscoll, was critically ill.

I went to his house to inquire for him but I was not allowed to see him. On the next day there was a sign on the door which said briefly, "Davey has not worsened." I thought of Davey all day and I hoped and prayed that he might get well. The following morning I ran up the hill to the Driscolls' house as soon as I awoke. I approached the door fearfully to read the small sign again. It stated simply, "Our Davey is safe in the arms of Jesus."

When I returned to St. Aiden's, I told Miss Giles that

I could not bear to look at the flower album Davey had given me when I left home and that I had put it away. Each time I thought of him, it was like a deep hurt. I could not believe that he was gone forever and that I would never see him again.

"You must expect these things, Freddy," she said. "We all lose a friend sometime. And what you feel is what we grownups call grief. It is all part of growing up, and by the look of your livery, you are doing so very rapidly. Bring it down to me this evening and I will lengthen the trousers for you."

Mr. Taylor must also have noticed that I was growing up. He said that I could take over his job of turning off the gas jets, and snuffing out the candles in the Chapel every evening after vespers. I was to lock up and bring him the key.

I didn't mind the task until the last gas jet was extinguished in the Chapel but after that I was in total, eerie darkness. I rushed out in the direction of the vestry, and as I reached the door, I looked back half-expecting to see some apparition. I ran breathlessly down the path to the kitchen as though the hobgoblins were still after me. When I handed Mr. Taylor the key, he looked at me and laughed.

"Freddy, it has taken me a long, long time to find out that there is one place that I can get you back from quickly! And now we have to prepare the rooms for the reunion. Go to Miss Giles' office and get your orders."

In the early summer, some of the graduates who had recently been given parishes of their own returned to St. Aiden's. Their reunion every two years took the form of a retreat; the whole week was observed in silence. Each night at dinner one of the graduates, seated alone at the end of a long refectory table, read from the Scriptures. The rest ate in silence and communed with God. It seemed odd not to hear the usual gay sounds of talk and laughter in the corridors and at the table. But after several days we did not feel it at all unnatural.

Then at the end of the retreat the silence ended abruptly, and everybody began to talk at once. The graduates were making up for lost time.

That year the Reverend Harding had decided to give a garden party to close the reunion. Mr. Taylor and Miss Giles were in charge of the arrangements. They assigned tasks to all of us, and to the extra servants who had been engaged to help with the service. A marquee was set up on the lawn for the luncheon, which was to be served out of doors. All of the people in the countryside and many distinguished friends of St. Aiden's were invited.

It was the grandest affair I had ever seen. I was allowed to help Mr. Taylor serve the port wine, and when no one was looking, I took a taste of it. It was delicious. In fact, it was so good that while I uncorked the bottles I drank three or four more glasses of the rich, heady port. I soon felt a warming glow of delight and elation, and I began to find everything and everybody at the party very amusing. I started to laugh and giggle. Suddenly I found myself cornered by Mr. Taylor, who seemed to appear out of thin air.

"I've been watching you," he said, "and I'd like to know what's so uncommonly funny?"

"I don't know, Mr. Taylor. Everything! Even you!"

"Is that so!" he said indignantly. "I'll tell you why you

think so—you're drunk! You young imp of Satan, you come with me!" He grabbed me by the scruff of the neck, took me to my room, and put me to bed.

The next evening, I went to see Miss Giles to apologize for my behavior at the party. Luckily for me, she was the only person in authority who saw my ignominious departure through the back of the marquee.

"I have been thinking about you since last night," she said, "and I believe you have learned about as much as we can teach you here as a page boy. You are like a colt in too small a pasture. You have been with us for more than two years and I think you should apply for a young-footman's job. If you wish, I will write to my friend, Miss Massey, who has an employment agency in Liverpool. I will recommend you highly and I am confident that she will find you a good job. It is her business to be on the lookout for personable young men who wish to go into domestic service."

"Miss Giles," I answered quickly, "I have been very happy here and I will be sorry to leave, but I would like that very much. I think I am too old now to be a page boy any longer."

A week later, a letter came from Miss Massey saying she had a job for me at the home of Squire Leache, Carden Park, in Cheshire. I was to come as soon as possible.

Mr. Taylor, Miss Giles, and Jane gave a party for me before I left. The old butler rose to drink a toast to my future and with fatherly admonition, he said:

"I drink to your health, Freddy, with only one glass of port, which must suffice to take care of all of your good luck."

Almost as I had come to St. Aiden's, so I left it. My tin trunk rested again on my shoulder, but I wore long trousers and a box coat had replaced the Eton jacket—the page boy had grown into the young-footman.

"I hope you will come back and see us," Miss Giles said, as she walked to the gate with me. "Write to me about your new job when you find time."

As I reached the first curve in the road, I looked back for one final glimpse of St. Aiden's. A small lady in a black dress with a lace collar, and her keys still hanging from her slim waist, was waving a little white handkerchief in parting.

CHAPTER

3

The Young-Footman

IT WAS drizzling as the trim luggage wagon drew away from the Carden depot. I put my coat collar around my neck to keep off the dampness and the chilling wind. I was sitting on the box next to the coachman, and he flicked his whip so that the idling horse would move faster. He didn't speak as we drove along and sat enveloped in his greatcoat like an old turtle drawn into his shell.

"Is it far to Carden Park?" I ventured.

"Not too far," he said, laconically. "About five miles."

In the last glimmer of the foggy evening light, the landscape looked unreal and ghostly. As we made our way through the lanes and turnings, the coachman didn't say another word and I was left to my own thoughts. I had started out from St. Aiden's that morning and taken the train at Birkenhead for Carden, seventy-five miles northeast of Liverpool. It had been a long journey and I had spent hours wondering about my new job. I felt like talking to someone—anyone.

"I beg your pardon, sir," I said to the coachman, "could you tell me what kind of a lady Mrs. Leache is?"

"Mrs. Leache, young man, is a very fine lady," he answered, "but she hasn't much to say."

"And Carden Park—is it very large?" I continued.

"Carden Park is one of the finest estates in the whole of Cheshire, the old Manor House is large enough and beautiful, too. But you'll find that it's a round of work to keep it that way." He chuckled to himself and drew back into his greatcoat again.

"And the Squire, sir, what is he like?"

"Ah, the Squire," and he lapsed into silence again.

"Yes," I persisted, "the Squire—what sort of man is he? Is it nice to work for him?"

"To tell you about the Squire would take a long time, lad. It's enough to begin with to tell you to do your job and see to it that you don't get under his feet. And he's not like Mrs. Leache—he talks a lot! Particularly about the things that don't suit his fancy. He'll let you know soon enough."

As the coachman finished this ominous statement, he pulled up the reins sharply. I saw that we had stopped before two great stone posts and that a large wrought-iron gate barred our way. Slowly a figure carrying a lantern came toward us.

"A fine night to be driving out, Charles. And who have you got there?"

"This is the new young-footman just arrived."

"I'm Freddy Gorst, sir," I said, "and I'm pleased to meet you."

"I'm Will Cotes, the head gardener, and that's the lodge

where I live, if you can see where the lights glow through the fog."

The gates closed behind us, and I noticed how bleak and tall the trees were which lined the drive. They touched each other high above us and formed a black arch as far ahead as I could see.

"That is only one of three gates to the Manor House," Charles said, "and there are two other lodges, the head game keeper's and the coachman's. That's mine, you know. And each one of us tends a gate. You might like to know it's about a mile from each gate to the house. We'll soon be there."

We passed a number of darkened buildings and finally drove into a large service court, which was bathed in shadowy light from the carriage lamps on either side of the door.

"Take your luggage out and follow me," Charles commanded. With a lantern held aloft over his head, he led me down a long corridor in the Service wing. After a very long walk, he knocked on a door and said,

"Are you there, Tom?"

"Righto, sir," a voice said as a touseled, red head came through the door. I saw a young boy, almost my own age, standing before me in a night shirt.

"Freddy, this is Tom Findley, the groom," the coachman said, "and you share this room with him. Here are your orders for the morning. Report to Mr. Ling, the butler, at seven-thirty in the main pantry. Good night and God rest you."

In the barnlike room which I shared with Tom, there seemed to be two of everything: two occupants, two fireplaces, two caned chairs, and two huge old four-poster beds from which the draperies had long since been removed. On my bed frame there were two gigantic feather beds onto which I climbed and tried to fall asleep. But the snores of my new roommate, and what I suspected was the patter of mice, kept me awake. I suppose one never sleeps soundly the first night in a strange place.

When I entered the pantry promptly at seven-thirty, the most elegant man I had ever seen was standing before me—Mr. Ling. I later learned that he had once been butler to the Prince of Wales, but right then he looked to me like the Prince of Wales himself! He wore striped trousers and a swallow-tailed coat, a fancy pearl-gray, satin vest, and black patent leather shoes. He continually fingered a gray silk four-in-hand tie, meticulously arranging the folds, and constantly appraising himself in a mirror on the wall.

"Good morning, Fred," he said. "You seem to have the virtue of punctuality. So far so good. Now, your first duty in the morning is to bring me my tea. At nine you will ring the bell for prayers. After breakfast you will wash the silver and glass. Then you will polish silver. You will relay all the fires, and you will back me up with the service at luncheon. Understood?"

"Yes, sir, Mr. Ling," I said, trying to remember all these duties.

"Now go and get your breakfast and report back to me so that I can measure you for a proper livery. We are going to have it tailored immediately; you can't very well serve in *that* outfit. . . ."

I went into the kitchen and I was shown to my place at the breakfast table by the housemaid. At the side of my plate, I found a horn filled with beer. Looking at it more closely, I realized that it was the antler of a stag which had been completely hollowed out and polished. I shuddered at the thought of beer for breakfast, and the maid must have read my mind.

"What are you looking at?" she said. "Don't you like your beer?"

"Well, I don't know," I replied, "I've never drunk beer for breakfast."

"What does *Your Majesty* usually have for breakfast?" she retorted.

"I would appreciate a cup of tea," I said hopefully.

"Tea?" she said scornfully. "You'd better drink your beer, because you're not going to get tea for breakfast here! The Squire don't allow it."

I did as I was told and went back somewhat unsteadily to the pantry to meet Mr. Ling, with the nasty taste of beer still in my mouth. I was to learn many things from Mr. Ling, the least of which was how to appreciate beer for breakfast. But at that moment he was more interested in the art of polishing silver.

"Now, this is what we do," Mr. Ling said. "We do it the old-fashioned way with Goddard's Powder, which I have sent up specially from London." He took off his coat, hung it up carefully, and put on a voluminous butler's apron which made him look like a huge, white pouter pigeon.

"We're ready," he continued. "Get the buckets of boiling water lined up. First, we will apply the powder, and after that you can rinse each piece in soap water and carefully dry it with those linen cloths that I have stacked for you on the shelf. Then you will work on the silver with the chamois. Pick out the finest grained ones, and be sure you wash them out after each use."

I spent the greater part of my first week at Carden Park polishing so much flat silver and so many table decorations that I had cramps in my fingers.

But I felt a great deal better when my livery finally came. It was a dress suit made of plum-colored wool with a matching vest trimmed with silver buttons. With it I wore my first dress shirt, a round collar, and a white piqué bow tie. I remembered my excitement when I first saw my page boy suit, but this was even finer and it fitted perfectly. But I didn't have long to admire myself, because Mr. Ling soon called me into the pantry.

"Fred," he said, "go upstairs to the Squire—he's in the second-floor study, and ask him for a drop of port for a special sauce which Cook is preparing for the sweet to-night. He keeps it locked up and we have to ask for it. He is very particular about his own sauces and garnishings. Just knock and enter, it's the custom."

I found my way to the entrance hall and I saw the beautiful double white stairway with its glowing mahogany handrail leading to the second floor. I climbed the right staircase, knocked softly on the first door, and entered.

The Squire was working at a large table desk writing in a ledger with a peacock quill. The tall wing chair in which he sat seemed to cramp his broad shoulders. As I entered he removed his pince-nez and looked up at me.

"Who are you?" he asked.

"I am Frederick Gorst, the new young-footman."

He looked me over from head to toe and said,

"Is that the livery Ling ordered for you? Turn slowly around. . . . It will do. Now, what do you wish?"

"Mrs. Perkins would like a drop of the special port."

"What!" he cried, jumping up from his chair, his face reddening and his jaw protruding far beyond his collar.

"Sir," he shouted, "how *dare* you ask for a *drop* of port! Who ever heard of a *drop* of port. Damn it, go out of this room and re-enter it and ask me for *some port!*"

I was frightened out of my wits but I repeated my entrance and timidly asked for *some port*. He listened attentively and then he looked up at me from under his heavy white eyebrows.

"Sir, what did you say your name was—Frederick?"

"Yes, Squire Leache, that is my first name."

"Have you any other names?"

"My middle name is John."

"That is what I shall have to call you. My son-in-law is called Frederick Hayes and that's enough Fredericks to have in one place at one time."

Clutching the bottle of port to me, I hurried back to the pantry. Mr. Ling was waiting for me and when he saw my distraught face, he said,

"What did the Squire say to you? You look as though you'd seen a banshee!"

"He said I'm no longer Fred—I'm *John!*" I gasped.

"Well, well! I think we'll take this fine old port," Mr. Ling chuckled, "and rechristen you."

That evening when work was over Mr. Ling did rechristen me. We were sitting in the pantry before the fire. Mr. Ling was in his chair with his accustomed horn of beer in hand.

"Will you have a horn, John?" he asked.

"No, thank you, sir. I don't think I will."

"Now, what is this, John, don't you really like beer?"

"Mr. Ling, I can't say I do or I don't. I have had so little of it to drink. I don't remember ever having it before I came here."

"We'll refresh your memory," he said slyly. "You try some and I'll give you a sixpence for every horn you drink."

I had four horns of cool beer and I earned two shillings. The money may have had something to do with it, but I decided that I liked the taste very much.

After two more, I found the courage to ask Mr. Ling a question that had been in my mind ever since I arrived.

"Sir," I said, "how does it happen that you have a Chinese name?"

"Everyone asks me that," he said, "but Ling is a very common name in England. It's possible that one of my ancestors went to China and liked the name better than his own and came home as Mr. Ling! Have some more beer, John, you're turning into quite a fellow."

Mr. Ling told me that a stag horn gave beer a flavor that was superior to any vintage champagne. While I couldn't savor this subtle difference because I had never tasted champagne, I took his word for it. By the time the evening ended, I certainly learned what "filling the horn" meant.

The next morning in the pantry, Mr. Ling asked me if I felt fit. Although I had a pounding headache, I said as cheerfully as I could, "Never better."

"Good! You'll be a man before you know it! And now I'll show you how we set the table. If you can master this folderol, you can set a table anywhere. I tell you, John, the Prince of Wales himself demanded less than the Squire does at dinner."

The dinner table was always laid with a thick baize underlining with a white damask cloth over it. Directly in the center of the table, Mr. Ling placed a large bowl of dark red geraniums which had been especially raised in the hothouse. Two silver baskets of fresh fruit and two pairs of five-branch candlesticks, with each candle covered by a fringed silk shade, made a lavish setting. Then the flat silver and the Crown Derby china with insets of the Squire's crest, the same lush red as the geraniums, were arranged for the service.

At Carden Park it was the custom for the flowers, fruit, and candles to remain on the table until just before the last course was served. Then Mr. Ling and I removed everything from the table. We stood with the damask cloth in our hands while the Squire said grace. Then he rose and took the end of the cloth nearest him, and he and Mr. Ling folded it into a neat square.

After this ritual was over, the table was dusted with a linen cloth, and the flowers, fruit, and candles were put back on the gleaming table top, along with the silver wine stands to hold the four port decanters with silver labels hanging from the neck of each one. Then the finger bowls on fruit plates were set before the guests. Each doilie under the finger bowls was a silken embroidery of a scene from the famous Carden Park Hunt.

In contrast to dinner, I was to learn that luncheon was quite a different sort of meal; it was completely informal. Both Mrs. Leache and Miss Gwendolyn wore tweeds. The

Squire favored knickerbockers and tweed shooting suits during the day, and heavy boots, that were kept as shiny as patent leather. He wore a stiff collar, and a black string tie. With this highly individualistic costume he preferred white, hand-made cambric shirts.

At luncheon everything was placed upon the table: bread, butter, entrées, side dishes, vegetables, and the desserts. Mr. Ling and I stood at our places while the family served themselves. However, there was one elegant touch —a silver filigree basket with exquisite flowers adorned the center of the table. Every morning the gardener brought in a tray of seasonal flowers from the greenhouse, and Mr. Ling worked over his arrangement like an artist before his canvas.

One morning, instead of bringing flowers, the gardener carried in a large basket that was carefully covered with vine leaves which he had meticulously tied on with raffia. At luncheon this was placed on the lace centerpiece instead of the customary silver flower basket.

When luncheon was over and I was clearing the table, I could no longer contain my curiosity. I peered into the basket and the perfect peaches lying under the leaves looked more like wax than real fruit. They were luscious! I took one and ate it, and it was so delectable that I continued to munch the stone to enjoy the flavor as long as I could. I was giving the lace centerpiece a final fold when I looked up, and Mrs. Leache was standing in the doorway.

What was I to do? How could I get rid of the peach stone? I couldn't throw it away, I couldn't chew it—there was only one thing to do, swallow it and choke if I had to! And this is exactly what I did. I thought what an ignoble end for the Squire's young-footman. Here lies Fred Gorst who died of a purloined peach! Mrs. Leache's expressionless, sad face suddenly became very animated and she almost shrieked,

"Whatever is the matter with you, John? You are *blue* in the face!"

I was choking but I had enough breath to gasp, "I'm—sorry, Madame. I—have—swallowed—a peach—stone!"

"What? Have you eaten one of the Squire's Persian peaches?" she cried.

"Yes, M'um, I have!"

"John, we must never, never let him know it! And now we have to do something about you!" She walked quickly to the door and pulled the bell cord, and in a few seconds Mr. Ling appeared as though he had sensed an emergency.

"Ling," she said, "take John to the pantry at once and give him all the bread he can eat, and a large dose of castor oil!"

As Mr. Ling led me into the pantry, I vowed that I would never eat stolen fruit again! By the end of the week I had added another resolution: I would never again eat stolen fowl.

The Squire's gardens covered an area of about ten acres. They were enclosed by a high, iron fence which kept out the roving deer, and any other intruders. Fairly close to the Manor House terrace was an extensive rose garden, and in the center of it an ancient stone well was surrounded by great old oaks. The Squire's golden pheasants roosted in them at night. He had trained his birds to come to the library window where he fed them every morning, and they arrived like clockwork. This was not entirely an act of altruism; each day he counted them there very carefully.

Mr. Ling was also a bird fancier but he preferred to eat them rather than look at them. The starlings and sparrows on the estate were in constant danger from his ingenious traps and snares. His latest invention was a masterpiece. He had devised a hand trap of two pliable willow poles about nine feet high with a fine-meshed net strung between them. However, this contraption required the services of two people. One snarer had to take a long wand and gently scare the bird off its perch into the net. When the hapless little creature flew into the net, the second snarer snapped the poles together and Mr. Ling had his victim. He would skin it with all the skill of a taxidermist, roast it, and eat it.

One evening, when Mr. Ling was sitting by the fireplace in the servants' dining room with Tom, the groom, and me, he nostalgically remarked that he hadn't eaten a bird in a long time. He said that he had watched a great flock of starlings roosting in the rose garden oaks at sunset, and that Tom and I would find it very easy to snare some with the new hand trap.

In the darkness, Tom and I went furtively and silently to the starling roost. I took the long wand to scare one of them into the trap which Tom grasped firmly in both his hands. I reached gently for the first bird perched on the nearest limb. Suddenly, something flew into the net, and as a raucous squawking began, we knew it could not be a starling.

"What is it, Tom?" I whispered.

"Dear God!" he said. "I think we've got a golden pheasant! We'd better kill it quick before somebody hears this racket."

And he took the poor bird out of the net and wrung its neck. I felt a bit sick.

When we came back to the house we presented the bird to Mr. Ling, who exclaimed in a loud voice:

"Heavens above! How did this happen? You've caught one of the Squire's golden pheasants!"

"It was an accident, Mr. Ling," I cried.

"Accident or no accident, we will never be able to explain it to the Squire. He will have our heads."

"What shall I do?" I asked anxiously. "Shall I bury it, sir?"

"Well, let's see—that might be one way to get rid of it, but I think I have a better method." And with a broad smile on his face, he said, "We'll eat it."

Mr. Ling skinned the bird quickly and precisely, and prepared it for the spit, which he slowly turned in the fireplace. As the aroma of the roasting bird filled the room, Mr. Ling was in a gourmet's paradise. The golden pheasant washed down with horns of beer was a feast fit for Squire Leache.

But the next morning was a time of reckoning. When the Squire counted his birds and the loss was discovered, Mr. Fendinck, the head gamekeeper, was immediately summoned. "Where is the twenty-fourth bird?" the Squire bawled.

Mr. Fendinck was a good huntsman and a good detective. He started his search at the roost where he found some tiny, tell-tale yellow and red feathers. Then he remembered Mr. Ling's fondness for roasted birds and he made straight for the pantry. When he arrived he asked Mr. Ling if, by the remotest chance, he had seen a stray golden pheasant.

Mr. Ling answered: "I wouldn't know a pheasant if it flew straight into that fireplace! But come, Fendinck, I see you so rarely—won't you join me in a little drink? How about a spot of whiskey?"

While Mr. Ling was pouring the drinks, Mr. Fendinck bent down, picked up some yellow feathers that were still lying on the hearth, and twirled them slowly around in his fingers.

"Very unusual starlings you've been eating, Ling," he said.

"This one *was* a bit odd," Mr. Ling said nonchalantly, "it had a long, yellow tail."

After he finished his whiskey, Mr. Fendinck dropped the feathers into the fireplace. "This seems like a good place for them," he said. "It also seems a shame that the Squire will never find his golden pheasant. Undoubtedly it just flew away—didn't like it here any more. But in the future, Ling, I suggest that you have your boys snare the more common starlings. There are dozens of the black variety in the garden. Pheasant could be a very costly dish for all of us. And by the way, I'd also be a bit more careful in the future where I got my whiskey! Good day!"

Carden Park

THE room in Carden Park which I admired most was the drawing room with its lifelike marble representations of the hunt overhanging the two great fireplaces, with tall windows and gold mirrors alternating between them.

It was appointed with priceless Queen Ann furniture covered in exquisite gold brocade matching the draperies. They cascaded from golden valances, which held them in place above the twenty-foot windows, to the floor where they were carefully arranged in fan pleats. These draperies were so fragile from age that they could not be dusted by hand. When Margaret, the parlormaid, cleaned them, she had to use a hand bellows to blow off the dust.

One morning as I was putting the Squire's silver snuff boxes back into their glass display case in the drawing room, Margaret, who was dusting in the anteroom, came dashing toward me and whispered,

"John! Come quickly! I have found a secret stairway to the cellar hidden in the floor!"

I ran into the anteroom with her—and lo and behold—a part of the flooring was tilted up like the lid of a box. Margaret had been dusting the paneling and had accidentally touched a knot in the wood which had released a cleverly concealed spring. Suddenly she had heard a creaking noise, and the planking had risen up on a chain from the floor.

I found a candle and looked down in the pitch darkness. All I could see was the outline of a stone stairway.

"Come on, Margaret," I said, "the family is out. Let's go down and see what's there! But you go first!"

Arming ourselves with heavy, silver candlesticks and tapers, we started down the winding staircase. When we reached the cellar, we came to a heavy, wooden door which swung open as we pushed against it. A smell of mustiness and dampness seeped through the doorway and utter blackness faced us. By the light of the candles we saw that we were in a circular room, which was filled with nothing more threatening than a long array of wine bins. We were finishing our inspection when I heard the Squire's booming voice.

"Who in the *devil's* down there?"

As Margaret and I emerged shamefacedly from the secret staircase, the Squire said angrily,

"John and Margaret, come into my study."

We followed him like lambs to the slaughter. He sat down at his desk and demanded an explanation.

Margaret stood up to him bravely. "Squire Leache," she said, "I had no intention of doing anything wrong. I was dusting in the anteroom and I touched something in the woodwork. The lid swung open from the floor and I was so frightened that I called John back from the drawing room. Curiosity, I guess, sir, got the better of us."

This simple and honest explanation seemed to soften the Squire and he told us that the secret room had been used as a hiding place for the priests during the Reformation. No one knew when the room was built nor how many hundreds of years it had been in use. The wine bins had been installed much later by the owner from whom his father had acquired Carden Park. Then he added sternly:

"But this I want clearly understood: no one is to go down into that cellar again. It is very dangerous. There are other hidden springs and passageways. Anyone who goes down there will be immediately discharged. That is all."

I wondered why the Squire was at times so irascible. But as the months went by, I traced the reason to the two things which he enjoyed more than anything in life—Cheshire cheese and port wine. This overindulgence had resulted in gout, so that he was periodically confined to Mrs. Leache's sitting room. He was forced to sit before the fire holding his bandaged foot upon a gout stool, specially designed for these painful occasions by a cabinetmaker. The top was shaped in a semi-oval so that the Squire's foot and the calf of his leg could rest comfortably upon it.

During these attacks of gout he was given to such fits of anger that almost everyone trembled in his presence—even his wife. He would shout and bellow at her with such ungovernable rage that the color would go from the poor lady's cheeks. We marveled how Mrs. Leache endured the Squire's fiendish tempers, but it was plain to see that her patience had long ago turned to resignation.

Whenever he was indisposed it was my duty to serve

the Squire's dinner on a small table in front of the constantly burning fire. One evening, when I came up to lay the table and see that everything was in readiness before I brought his tray from the pantry, he ordered me to get him a whiskey and seltzer.

In those days, seltzer bottles were corked and sealed in the same manner that champagne bottles are today. I always carried a small pair of scissors to cut the wires, which were difficult to remove by hand. So now I poured the whiskey into the glass and prepared to open the seltzer bottle, carefully cutting the wires. Suddenly the Squire shouted at the top of his lungs,

"What in God's name do you think you're doing? You're going to let that bottle explode in my face—you young fool!"

He stood up in his chair and, without thinking, pounded his foot down on the floor. He howled as his weight settled on his gouty foot, and in a voice that could be heard in the gamekeeper's lodge, he cursed his fate and me. I was so frightened that I ran trembling from the room. When I reached the pantry and described the incident, Mr. Ling laughed. "Don't let the old blighter scare you," he said, quite unimpressed by my adventure. "He's just a big bag of hot air."

Mr. Ling was the only member of the household who was never afraid of the Squire. Mr. Ling had run the Manor House for many years with a firm and secure hand, and knew that the Squire couldn't get along without him.

Every week Mr. Ling was accustomed to go to Chester by train, a distance of about fifty miles. He left early Wednesday morning and returned late Thursday afternoon at teatime. He always brought back a large quantity of fish and, in the absence of ice to preserve it, the fish was wrapped in a bundle of heavy, brown paper and cloth. But one Thursday, fish was not the only thing that Mr. Ling brought back!

When he entered the kitchen with his large parcel, he staggered happily under its weight. But when he put down the parcel I noticed that he was really in the throes of another kind of vertigo. Mr. Ling was completely and delightfully drunk. I suggested that I would gladly serve the dinner and that he might like to go to bed, but he said, "Freddy, my boy, the motto of my family is 'Never falter —no matter how much you've worshipped at the Shrine of Bacchus—carry on!' "

But from the moment that Mr. Ling entered the dining room to serve dinner, it was obvious that he couldn't carry a teacup. He dropped silver, china—everything that he held in his hands slipped away. I watched the Squire out of the corner of my eye, and I knew that he would soon diagnose Mr. Ling's condition. I was right. Almost immediately, as though he were conducting a meeting, Squire Leache rapped on his crystal glass with a knife.

"Ling," he said in a voice that vibrated with rage, "you will leave the dining room at once and go to your own quarters. John will finish serving our dinner."

I took over and, for my first solo performance, managed very well. When I returned to the pantry once dinner was over, I found Mr. Ling sobering up on beer. After these additional drinks, which he said "always cleared his head nicely for the morning," he bade me a dignified "good night" and went quietly to bed.

Early in the morning the Squire rang for Mr. Ling. Mr. Ling was in the Squire's study for such a long time that I feared something drastic must be happening. When he returned to the pantry almost an hour later, he sat down in his chair and stared moodily into space.

"Mr. Ling," I said anxiously, "what has happened? Did the Squire discharge you?"

"Of course not, John. The Squire wouldn't sack me. He just delivered a lecture on the effects and evils of drink. He himself has a profound knowledge of the subject. To-day he was so carried away by the beauty of his own words, that the tears began to run down his cheeks. I'm sure if you go up to the study, you'll find him still crying."

The Squire must have recovered rapidly from his own oration on self-denial, because a few minutes later Mrs. Leache ordered me to announce to the household, when I made my rounds ringing the handbell for prayers, that the Squire would preach a special sermon on insobriety.

By five minutes of nine, almost everyone on the estate had arrived: the family, Mr. Ling, the cook, Margaret, the coachman, the head gamekeeper, the head gardener and all of his assistants, the groom, the housemaids, the scullery maid, the ladies' maids, the strapper, the stable boy, and some of the estate families—even the laundry maids came to prayers that day. This large attendance was easily explained. Everybody expected a good show because the news of Mr. Ling's lapse from grace had traveled like a brush fire across the estate.

Morning prayers were always conducted in the Long Hall. A beautiful thirteenth century, stained-glass window gave it the atmosphere of a private chapel. The ceiling was a series of square panels of carved flower wreaths, and the paneled walls were dark from age and many waxings. In the center of the Hall was a long oak table supported by massive carved griffons.

On it stood the famous Carden Park cheese cradle, which was removed only for prayers. The Squire had received many offers from antique collectors for this unusual piece, and it always seemed to me that when his prayer book and Bible replaced the cheese cradle, he was putting aside all worldly temptations so that he could keep his mind on divine services.

First Mrs. Leache and Miss Gwendolyn took their places. They sat in the tall, wooden chairs nearest to the table, and the rest of the household sat in the chairs which lined both sides of the Hall. When the Squire made his entrance from the library, everyone rose. All eyes followed him as he walked to his chair. He stood behind it for a moment in meditation, his eyes turned upward as if in communion with the heavenly hosts. Then he lowered his head and said, "Amen." After that he carefully arranged the folds of his coat and pulled back his chair.

But now as he slowly sat down, the chair suddenly gave way and in an instant he was sprawling grotesquely on the floor. While he struggled to his feet, a piercing, girlish giggle broke the tense silence of the room.

"You damned silly housemaid!" he shrieked. "Be quiet! Someone get me a chair!"

I ran to get one and I held it firmly for him as he sat down. When at last he was comfortable he said, "Now, let us pray."

After he read the Twenty-third Psalm, his voice grew

gradually more and more indistinct. He ended the Lord's Prayer in almost a whisper and shortly concluded the service. The gathered household was intensely disappointed, but Mr. Ling was very relieved because he had expected a public denunciation.

Later we all learned that the Squire had painfully injured his back when he had fallen and was unable to deliver the sermon he had planned. I was secretly convinced that the Squire's chair had collapsed by an act of God, who, I might say, seemed to prefer Mr. Ling's occasional, frank enjoyment of the cup to Squire Leache's habitual wine bibbing.

The Squire was an egotistical, cantankerous old man who lorded it over both his family and his servants. Like all hypocrites he was very demanding, critical of everyone, and extremely self-indulgent. So when the Squire had a "comeuppance," there was quiet but general rejoicing. The opening hunt of the season provided the gentry, the farmers, and even the Squire's staff with the opportunity to enjoy a local joke at Squire Leache's expense.

In the course of the three years that I served at Carden Park, I had seen the famous Carden Park foxhounds once each year. When the Squire came into the estate, he did not want the outstanding pack of hounds which had belonged to his father. He presented them to Sir Watkins William Wynn, his neighbor, because he himself loathed and detested dogs. He disliked hearing them bark, he detested hearing them sniff—in short—he hated them. He would not allow a dog in the house! So when Sir William, out of gratefulness for this munificent gift, suggested that the first meet of the hunting season should be held at

Carden Park to continue the tradition of the Carden Park Pack, it was an honor with which the Squire could have happily dispensed.

A few days before the meet, Squire Leache called in Mr. Fendinck, the head gamekeeper, to give his orders. Even though the idea of a fox hunt was anathema to the Squire, he went about the estate planning for it with his usual attention to details. He was conscious of his position in the countryside, and since this was a great social event, proper preparations had to be made.

In the wilder portions of the Squire's property there were coverts, little woody copses, where the gamekeepers raised pheasants and partridges. The foxes' holes were near these coverts, and they made off with the birds whenever they had the chance. The Squire ordered Mr. Fendinck to see that all of the fox holes were blocked off by the earth-stoppers, a group of local farmers responsible for blocking up the fox holes before each hunt. If they did their job thoroughly, there would be only one fox in the field, and the dogs would not go astray following more than one scent.

The morning of the hunt at a little after ten, the gentry rode up to the front entrance of the Manor House. The Squire and Mrs. Leache welcomed and greeted them as they assembled.

The ladies were attired in colorful habits of hunter green, purple, and black. They all rode side-saddle and wore straight skirts with knickers underneath. Their skirts were only fastened on one side and draped down smartly from the saddles of their horses. All of them had on silk top hats or black derbies, and flattering veils closely tied to keep their hair from blowing.

The gentlemen were even more spectacular in white buckskin breeches, black riding boots, and scarlet coats. They wore black velvet jockey caps which set off their flamboyant costumes. The Master of the Hounds was dressed in the same fashion except for a scarlet jockey cap, an extra mark of distinction.

When the entire hunt was assembled, the hunting horn was blown by a special groom. It was a most joyful sound and it electrified the riders and their horses, and even the dogs sensed that the hunt had begun. The chase was on!

The Master of the Hounds and the pack moved off to covert to draw the fox. The ladies and gentlemen followed a short distance behind, waiting for the signal, the excited cries of the hounds giving chase. As soon as the last rider was out of earshot, Squire Leache turned to Mr. Ling and me and said:

"Thank God! That's over! Now we won't have any more of those damn baying, yelping hound dogs about for quite some time! Not for a whole year! Those idiots out there—riding all over my land, knocking down my fences, breaking their bloody necks! . . . 'Tally-ho' . . . damn fools. . . ." Still muttering to himself, he stomped into the house and retired to his study. Heaven help anyone who crossed him on the opening day of the hunting season!

And in this particular meet, heaven helped the hunted. We learned later that the earth-stoppers had not properly blocked up all the fox holes. Seven foxes were drawn from one covert alone, thus dividing the hunt and almost turning it into a shambles. The riders became holpelessly confused, and they rode off in all directions chasing seven foxes at once.

After a while the error was discovered, and the Master of the Hunt directed the riders to pursue one fox, which was finally brought to ground. The first lady in at the kill received the tail, or the brush, as it is called, and the first gentleman rider in was rewarded with the head. The rest of the fox was cast to the dogs. To the victor belong the spoils!

This meet was the subject of much merriment. At the end of the hunting season, the earth-stoppers gave a dinner at the village inn, "The Cock of Barton." Although it reflected unfavorably on their professional abilities, it gave the earth-stoppers a good deal of malicious pleasure to recall the hunt in which they had allowed seven foxes to be drawn from Squire Leache's coverts. And it was said in the countryside that this evening was particularly memorable, because they toasted the Squire, the Carden Park hounds, and each of the seven foxes!

Exciting and colorful as the hunting season was, the most joyful and festive of all occasions at Carden Park was Christmas. Each yuletide the Squire and Mrs. Leache gave a wonderful Christmas party for the servants and their families.

We all gathered in the Great Hall at eleven o'clock Christmas morning for prayers, which the Squire conducted. Then we stood in line and passed before the Squire and Mrs. Leache, who presented each of us with a sovereign and wished us all a Merry Christmas. I had already received a gift of three pounds which Mrs. Leache had previously presented to me, so I felt wealthy and full of good cheer.

All of the staff on the estate had been invited to the Christmas dinner, which was given in the servants' dining room in the Manor House. The gardeners had decorated the room and the fireplace with boughs of evergreen and holly. There was an enormous kettle hanging from a huge hook in the fireplace. It was about four feet in diameter and filled with hot beer, to which nutmeg, Jamaica ginger, cloves, and cinnamon sticks were being contantly added. This brew was kept simmering, but not allowed to come to a boil. All day long we kept replenishing the beer grog, and everyone filled his horn.

Four long tables and wooden benches had been set up for the dinner, which was served at one o'clock. First, a great hog's head, stuffed with sausage meat and pâté de foie gras from the Squire's own geese, was carried in by four men and set upon a separate table. It had a shiny red apple in its mouth and the ferns and greens which decorated the huge board lent a pagan touch. Then came the cold meats and roasts. The main dish consisted of the finest joints of beef and Yorkshire pudding, and many kinds of vegetables. There were liberal helpings of English mustard with the beef on this Christmas day! And finally, the plum pudding was brought in, burning and flaming with brandy.

The feast lasted for most of the afternoon and by the time everyone had left the servants' hall of the Manor House, Mr. Ling and I were almost too tired to serve Christmas dinner for the family and their guests.

They dined at eight o'clock, and their dinner beginning with soup and ending with plum pudding, mince pies, trifle pudding, and the Squire's favorite Cheshire cheese, was exactly like the servants' feast, except that sherry wine was served with the soup, Rhine wine with the fish, Burgundy with the meat, claret with the salad, champagne with the dessert, and port wine with the cheese.

Coffee followed in the small, upstairs sitting room. When I took the coffee tray up, Mr. Frederick Hayes, the Squire's son-in-law, was waiting for me at the top of the stairs. I was curious to meet him because it was on his account that I was called John by the Squire.

"John," he said, coming bluntly to the point, "this may not be exactly the proper time to bring this matter up, but Mrs. Hayes and I would like to have you come to Ashton-Hayes as single-footman. You have done well here and you could gradually take over most of the responsibilities of Powell, our butler, who is now quite old. We intend to pension him soon, and then you would head the staff as first footman. I have spoken to the Squire and he agrees that you can come back to Ashton-Hayes with us. I will give you twenty-five pounds a year which is five pounds more than you are earning now."

"Mr. Hayes," I said at once, "thank you for your kind offer. May I think it over and give you my answer in a few days?"

When I discussed Mr. Hayes' offer with Mr. Ling, he was most encouraging. He felt that I had learned everything that was required to be a competent single-footman.

"My dear boy," he said, "if you can survive three years in the service of Squire Leache, you can wait on the Devil himself and find it easier!"

If Mr. Ling intended this jest as a flattering testimonial,

I was willing to accept it as such. But I knew very well that he would spend the rest of his days with the Squire.

When I left Carden Park, Mrs. Leache kindly presented me with a small, silver snuff box, a memento of the faithful performance of my duties. Then she added a little sadly, "And I do hope you will forget the times when the Squire lost his temper. He really doesn't mean half of what he says!"

5

Sea Voyage

WHEN I left Squire Leache's employ, I had been well trained as a young-footman. I was serious-minded and knew everything about polishing silver, faultlessly serving a dinner or handing a tray. I performed all of the functions of a footman like a puppet on a string. I could run any household perfectly, but I knew very little about the world outside, or how young people should enjoy themselves.

Then one morning, after I had served Mr. and Mrs. Hayes for six months, I got up at the usual time—at five-thirty—dressed, and went to the kitchen for breakfast. While I was having my coffee, the room suddenly started to spin around and I fainted.

When I came to, I found myself on my bed where Mr. Powell, the butler, and some of the other members of the staff had taken me. The doctor came and his diagnosis was swift and simple. He said I was suffering from exhaustion.

It was no wonder that I could no longer keep up the

pace that was required at Ashton-Hayes; I had worked from early morning until eleven at night almost without a pause. It was as though Mr. Hayes thought his servants were automatons made of iron and steel.

Dr. Burton asked me how much time I had off for rest and recreation, and I told him that I had not had a day off since I began to work at Ashton-Hayes six months ago. Moreover, I had not had a holiday nor seen my family in more than three years. He shook his head in disbelief, and said:

"John, this is a very serious matter. How old are you?"

"I'm almost eighteen, Dr. Burton," I said.

"You are very tall for your age, and your pale complexion leads me to believe that you need some sunshine and fresh air. Tell me," he added thoughtfully, "have you ever been to sea?"

"When I was a small boy, Dr. Burton, I used to sail with my father," I said.

"Then what I have to suggest may not be so drastic. I want you to have a rest for several weeks, and then I want you to get a job at sea. If you don't do this immediately, I will not be responsible. I will speak to Mr. Hayes myself."

I had no idea that I was so ill. But now I was alarmed and decided to follow the doctor's instructions.

Dr. Burton was a man of his word, and Mr. Hayes could not have been more shocked when he heard the truth. He gave me a letter to Mr. Ismay, an official of the White Star Line, and shortly afterwards I left for several weeks' rest and a holiday with my family in Liverpool.

I had almost forgotten what it was like to be with them, to roam about freely, strolling in the streets of Liverpool, looking in the shop windows, and having tea served to me by my doting sisters. It was wonderful to feel their love and concern, and Mama told me over and over again how much I had helped her to provide for the younger children, but that she had no idea I had been working so hard. I reassured her that even though I was now six feet two inches tall and as thin as a walking-stick, I would survive. The sea and the salt air would certainly restore my health.

After two weeks at home, I went to the offices of the White Star Line to see Mr. Ismay and present my letter from Mr. Hayes. He advised me to start in the steerage for my first sea voyage, and promised that I would be promoted to the saloon class stewards at the earliest opportunity.

I was assigned to the "Germanic," one of the "floating palaces" of the White Star Line. Mr. Ismay told me that she once had held the world's record for the fastest Atlantic crossing: 7 days, 11 hours, and 37 minutes from New York to Queenstown.

I often recall that old ship, which was then considered so swift and well appointed. I wonder what the passengers on the great liners of today would think of her, with all the speed and comfort that is now provided. I'm afraid the "Germanic" would hardly be considered a luxury liner compared to the "Queen Elizabeth" or the "United States." But when I boarded her, and inspected the oak-paneled saloons and dining room, I was positive that there was no finer ship afloat.

The day I sailed from Liverpool, my parents and my sister Lily came to see me off. I can still see them waving to me from the pier. Lily's imploring look and Mama's sad face are etched in my memory. They were fearful that I would never return, although I had given them my solemn promise that I would not stay in America.

I was on the Mersey River again, sailing into the Irish Sea. I looked back at the shore, at the little dock where Papa had kept his fishing smack, but from the deck of the "Germanic" the scenes of my boyhood seemed strange and different. The great ship nosed her way slowly into the open waters for the port of Queenstown in Ireland, and my reveries were soon lost in a host of duties.

The first job I had was to help throw over the side all the old straw mattresses from the last voyage. I was assigned to clear them out of a storeroom which was right over the propeller, and there wasn't a breath of air in that dank, straw-filled room. Each time the propeller came out of the water, the whole ship creaked and shook. The sea was running high and the "Germanic" started to roll and toss. I began to have butterflies in my stomach and I hurried to the deck for some fresh air. An old seaman lumbered toward me and gave me a resounding slap on the back.

"What's the matter—are you seasick?" he inquired politely.

"Yes, I suppose I am," I said clutching the rail. "I think I'm going to die!"

"You won't die," he said and then he lowered a pail on a rope into the sea. When he hauled it back, he handed me a ladle full of sea water and told me to "drink her down." I hoped there might be some magic cure in swallowing some of it. Actually the briny potion was much worse than I expected, but the immediate results delighted the seaman.

"You'll be all right now," he said. "And another thing

my lad, keep busy. Work takes your mind off it. It's the best remedy for what you've got, and you'd better have your sea legs by tomorrow. We're running into some mighty dirty weather."

The next day was rainy and blustery. The sea and the sky seemed to merge into a leaden grayness. At Queenstown we took on two hundred and fifty Irish girls who were emigrating to America to seek domestic employment. They came aboard laughing and excited, loaded down with valises and colorful paper boxes which we carried to their quarters in the steerage, the lowest deck below the water line.

I was quite pleased with this assignment because I had never seen so many pretty girls at one time, and I looked forward to meeting some of them during the voyage. But I had to wait four days before any of them appeared on deck again.

The storm broke in all its fury as Queenstown slipped over the horizon. Luckily I had my sea legs now, and I was able to go about my duties. The poor Irish colleens were not so fortunate. They were confined to their bunks and all of them were violently ill from the pitching and wallowing motion. They occupied double bunks of canvas which were roped onto iron posts that had been installed into the floor. Each one had a straw mattress, the only bedding that was supplied for the entire voyage. I could not imagine a more pathetic and oppressive sight than all those poor seasick girls lying on their hammocks in that miserable, airless, and overcrowded room.

Occasionally, we were ordered to set up a funnel, leading from an upper deck to the steerage, to provide some fresh air and ventilation. I had heard that the steerage accommodations were far from pleasant but I could hardly believe that human beings could be subjected to such indignities. They were herded in like cattle. But I also learned that the recuperative powers of my "fellow women" were enormous.

The fifth morning at sea the sun was shining again, and the Atlantic Ocean was serene and sparkling. The stewards were ordered to lash barrels of hardtack to the ship's rail on the steerage deck. It was amusing for us to watch the young Irish girls, still looking pale and wan, straggle onto the deck. They would stare longingly at the biscuits, walk away a few steps while they were debating whether or not to eat, and then turn back and quickly take one out of the barrel. They nibbled gingerly at the first one, but they seemed to enjoy the second helping. The hardtack was followed by smoked herring which was served to them that night at supper. They ate this sparingly, too, at first, but the salty taste soon whetted their appetites. All of them seemed to be very happy just to be hungry and on deck again. As they regained their strength, they became gay and lively once more.

The last night of the voyage, the Chief Steward, Mr. Jamison, gave a party for all the steerage passengers. Some of the Irish girls did spirited jigs for us, and some of the sailors reciprocated with hornpipes. The last part of the evening was devoted to the Irish reel, which I watched with great pleasure. A young lady, Sheila O'Shaughnessy, asked me to dance, something which I had never done before, and we went out onto a corner of the dance floor. I confessed my ignorance, so she taught me some of the simple figures.

After I had mastered them, we were able to join the other couples in a "right and left." At midnight this pleasant evening ended. We sang "God Save the Queen" and wished all the emigrants "Good Luck in America."

After we docked in New York, the stewards were given shore leave and two dollars for spending money. Fortunately, I had a little more than that because I had earned a pound and ten shillings watching over two children for a lady traveling first class who was too ill to follow her active youngsters around the decks. Her generosity enabled me to go to the pubs and see the sights with my friends.

Most of the British sailors who went ashore in New York patronized Tom Sharkey's Saloon. He had retired from prizefighting but his establishment still retained the flavor of his former glory. In the back room, a ring had been set up on a huge stage, which was called "Sharkey's Squared Circle," and here bouts were put on every night. The hundreds of seamen who watched the fights drank vast quantities of beer drawn from the countless barrels stacked along the walls. There were sailors from every ship in the harbor and there was many a boisterous reunion; tales of voyages and experiences at sea were exchanged far into the night.

With my limited resources I had to be careful not to spend all of my money at once. I wanted to see New York, so I rode everywhere on the street cars. I was told to go to the Eden Musée, or "Mewsey," as the sailors called it. They had described it as one of the wonders of New York, but I found it to be just another waxworks collection on a larger scale than the circus in Liverpool.

Nevertheless I was thrilled by the activity and bustle of

the city. Everybody seemed busy. New York was all so new and full of youthful vitality compared to the staid, old world from which I had come. What impressed me most was the heartiness and friendliness of the people I met. There were many nationalities who seemed to have kept the flavor of their homelands, but I noticed that some other leavening ingredient had been added.

I began to understand that their open-heartedness was based on a feeling of mutual equality. I realized that I had worked in an atmosphere of rigid class distinction all of my life and I had passively accepted my lot without ever questioning whether it was right or wrong. For the first time I was seeing something quite different—here was something to make any young Englishman marvel: there was an equal opportunity in America for everyone.

When it was time for the "Germanic" to make her return voyage to Liverpool, she had been completely restocked. Mr. Jamison, the chief steward, called me to his office and told me that I had been made a saloon steward. This was welcome news. I don't think I would have survived if I had remained in the steerage. It was anything but the ideal place for a health cure.

Mr. Jamison was exceptionally kind to me and he singled me out from the other younger members of the crew. I had never met a man who had as much responsibility as he did, and who directed so many people in so many diverse tasks with such quiet efficiency. He said that I had been assigned to the steerage to try my mettle and that I had passed the initial test. Because he knew that I had been a footman, he felt that I would soon learn how the kitchens, dining rooms, and saloons were run. He urged me to work my way up on the ship's staff and consider the sea as a life work.

I spent several evenings with Mr. Jamison in his quarters and he told me that he had never regretted his choice of a vocation. Even though his job was confining, his quarters small, and if he wanted to go for a walk he had to do his turns around the deck, there were compensations. "The sea is different every day," he said, "and there is a kind of peace and freedom here you never find ashore."

Mr. Jamison's influence remained with me for many years, long after his untimely death. He died on duty when his ship, on her maiden voyage, April 14, 1912, struck an iceberg off Newfoundland. The name of the ship still fills me with sadness whenever I hear it—the S.S. "Titanic."

When we finally completed our voyage and docked in Liverpool, I returned home and told my family about my experiences. I talked with such enthusiasm about America at a Saturday night gathering before the kitchen fire that my father turned to me and said:

"Frederick, I have always wanted to return to America. I have wanted to go back there ever since I was a boy—perhaps you have it in your blood!"

He told us the story of his voyage on the first sidewheel steamer, the "Kangaroo," which took forty days to make the crossing to Canada. My grandparents had to take their own bedding, mattresses, blankets, and most of their own food which they prepared themselves on the ship. From Montreal they traveled by train and wagon to a ranch in Ontario, near the American border, where they lived and worked. After many years my grandfather returned to England to spend the remainder of his life in Lancaster.

Here he went into the grocery business, and in time became prosperous, and an outstanding citizen. He was appointed the governor, or chief warden, of Lancaster Prison.

When Grandfather died, he left a sizeable estate. His legacy to my father included his gold watch and chain, which had been a gift from the town of Lancaster for his public service. It was a fine old timepiece with a tiny chime and a jeweled face.

My father presented this watch to me while I was at home. Although I knew that Papa had too much tact to put it into words, this gift was in effect a bestowal on a favorite son. I felt very grown-up and important when I linked the gold chain through my vest and put the watch in a small upper pocket. From that moment on, I unbuttoned my coat, took out the watch, and consulted it twenty times a day. It became the mark of my father's faith in me, and I vowed that I would guard it carefully, and keep it always. But I could not foretell the future.

On my fourth voyage to America, I shared a bunk with a young man, one of the assistant cooks. One morning, when I reported to Mr. Jamison's office for my orders, I remembered that I left my watch under my pillow. I asked for permission to get it. When I returned to the "glory hole," it was not under my pillow, and after searching through all of my possessions, I had to face the fact that it was gone. I asked the young cook if he had seen it, and he replied that he knew nothing about it. When I returned to Mr. Jamison's office, I told him I couldn't find it anywhere. He waited a moment, and then replied decisively,

"Come on, Fred. I think we'll see about this right now. We'll have a little talk with your bunkmate."

As we entered the bunkroom, the young cook was standing by the open porthole and it was obvious, because of his guilty look, that he had just thrown something over the side. After Mr. Jamison vigorously cross-examined him, he broke down and admitted that he had taken my watch. He said that he felt trapped and frightened, and in his panic he decided to drop it into the sea. I was inconsolable about the loss and every time I looked at the ocean I thought of the watch lying at the bottom, ticking away its final hours in the timeless depths.

I never understood why this young chap behaved in this way, and what motivated his mean and spiteful act. It was no consolation to know that he had never stolen anything before. I was so upset by the incident that when we arrived in New York, I sent a cable to Miss Massey in Liverpool and asked her to have a job waiting when I returned. Somehow I was no longer interested in remaining at sea.

As soon as we docked in Liverpool, I went to see Miss Massey at her employment office.

She was a jovial young lady with an efficient and businesslike air. It was rather unusual to see a woman occupying a position normally held by a man. She greeted me cheerfully and told me that she still remembered the letter Miss Giles had written about me more than four years ago from St. Aiden's. Then she added that my services at Squire Leache's had been completely satisfactory.

"And now, Fred," she said, "let me reply to your cablegram in person. I have an excellent job for you if you want it. It is at Court Hey, the residence of Mr. Walter and Mr. Richard Gladstone, the nephews of the former Prime Minister, William Ewart Gladstone. You are to serve as first footman under Mr. Downes, the butler, and Mrs. Swan, the cook, who is really the head of the household. They are offering fifty pounds a year. Could you be ready by tomorrow?"

"Miss Massey," I replied eagerly, and to the point, "I am ready now."

The First Footman

COURT HEY, the handsome Georgian residence of Mr. Walter and Mr. Richard Gladstone, stood on a gently sloping knoll with an unbroken view to box-hedged gardens, terraces, ornamental trees, and lawns which stretched like a perfect carpet to the encircling meadows. The house had been built with great taste and care by Mr. Robertson Gladstone, the father of the two gentlemen who now occupied it. The white limestone had weathered very prettily, and the luxuriant ivy which covered the walls of the house and gardens had been so carefully tended for so many years that it was like a warm, green blanket enfolding the house in its surroundings.

The gravel drive from the main gates wove its way toward the entrance of the house through the park of fine old elms, cedars, and oaks. An imposing white porte-cochère covered the driveway where it formed a circular terrace and turned around the house to the back service court. There was another drive which entered the estate from the rear gates and this approach traversed the area of the orchards, stables, extensive greenhouses, and the large kitchen gardens.

Mr. Richard and Mr. Walter Gladstone always used the rear-entrance gate when they left or returned to Court Hey separately. Each had his own coachman and his own carriage, which was driven to the stable yard where he alighted. Then each one walked the three hundred yards to the house and entered by the service court door leading to the kitchen hall. It was a custom, rain or shine, to enter the house in this fashion. It was also customary that no one, except the guests who came once a week for Sunday dinner, used the front entrance.

Mr. Richard and Mr. Walter Gladstone entered the house by the kitchen in order to chat with Mrs. Swan, the cook-housekeeper, the main cog in the wheels which turned so smoothly and efficiently in this elegant establishment. Invariably every afternoon, Mr. Richard Gladstone arrived first.

Mr. Richard Gladstone was a man in his early sixties. He was markedly blond, florid, and clean shaven. He always disguised his paralyzed right arm by holding it close to his side.

As he entered, his greeting was always the same.

"Good afternoon, Mrs. Swan," he would inquire, "what kind of day has it been for you?"

And Mrs. Swan's answer never varied. "Good afternoon, sir. It's been a usual day." No one felt the need for any originality in these simple salutations. But one day when I was in the kitchen, Mr. Gladstone seemed perturbed as he entered.

"Has Mercer's finally sent that order of chablis?" he asked rather sharply.

"Yes, sir," she replied. "The dray from Mercer's come this mornin' from Liverpool with a dozen cases of wine ye ordered and it is already stored away in your cellar. Mr. Richard, I selected one bottle at random to try it for your fish sauce this evenin'. I hope it meets with your approval, sir."

As Mrs. Swan spoke, each successive "r" whirred sharply into the air. She had such a thick Scotch burr that it sounded as though her tongue were covered with thistles.

"Good, Mrs. Swan, good indeed. I look forward to it with pleasure," Mr. Richard said.

Then he bowed ceremoniously and left the kitchen to go to his rooms.

Mr. Walter always arrived later. In contrast to his brother, he was several inches taller, about five years older, and his pale face was framed by "Imperial whiskers," a style of beard that came to a point on his chin. This adornment was popular in the early Victorian era, and his clothes too seemed faintly old-fashioned.

His conversation with Mrs. Swan was an echo of his brother's: a greeting, an inquiry for her health, and an interrogation about the wine *he* had ordered. You could be sure that he had chosen red, if Mr. Richard had selected white. The gentlemen stored their imported vintages in separate wine cellars, subterraneously built so the temperature would be constant and cool.

Mrs. Swan had been in the employ of the Gladstone family for thirty-six years when I came there. She was now no longer young although her energy belied it. Everything was planned to make her work as light as possible. All of us assisted in the kitchen: Mr. Downes, the butler; Wilson, the second footman; Thornhill, the page boy; the head kitchenmaid and the scullery maid washed every dish, pot, and bowl that Mrs. Swan used in creating her culinary works of art.

I enjoyed helping her because she was such a superb cook. She willingly relinquished some of her minor tasks, but she was still the taskmistress and she had never given up any of her power as head stewardess of her kitchen kingdom. This was the only household in which I ever served where the cook managed the menus, the supplies, and even the accounts, which she rendered directly to the estate agents in Liverpool.

Over the years, the Gladstone family had entrusted her with the management of their entire domestic establishment. Even Mr. Downes, who had been at Court Hey for over twenty years and now acted as Mr. Walter's valet as well as butler, was still regarded as something of a newcomer because of Mrs. Swan's great seniority. He did, however, have complete charge of ordering the beer for the staff, which gave him some importance among us.

I was now a first footman and I was delighted with my new position. I was able to enjoy my duties because I really knew my job. I performed them automatically and effortlessly—the work seemed comparatively easy. I gave orders to Wilson, the second footman, and young Thorny, the little page, and I enjoyed having two helpers who performed the more menial jobs, although I never took advantage of their willingness and good nature.

My own duties began at seven o'clock in the morning.

At seven-thirty I awakened Mr. Richard and Mr. Walter. It was Mr. Walter's habit to start the day with a special concoction. At seven each morning, when I came into the kitchen, I was greeted by the head dairyman with:

"Gorst, I've been waiting for you. You're three minutes late, and this milk is cooling off. Get on with it, or Mr. Walter's grog will be cold!"

Technically he was wrong: grog is a drink of spirits and hot water thoroughly mixed. According to the parts of water added to the whiskey or rum, it was called *two*-water grog, or *three*-water grog. But I never corrected him because the word sufficed to describe this early-morning beverage which I preferred to think of as "Mr. Walter's toddy." The milk which the dairyman brought had to be still warm from the cow. Into five gills of milk I poured three gills of the finest West Indian rum from a bottle which was never less than a hundred years old. Then I hurried up the stairs, with the quart glass completely swaddled in a tea cosey. I knocked, entered, opened the blinds, and addressed him:

"A very good morning, sir. Your milk is ready."

"Good morning, Gorst. What kind of a day is it?"

I gave the weather report while Mr. Walter drank his milk in almost one draught. A moment later, Downes entered to assist Mr. Walter with his toilette. Everything went like clockwork in this household.

I left to lay the table for breakfast so that the service would be in readiness for Mr. Walter, who came down first. Wilson and Thorny had already prepared the hot plate which was kept going with methylated stoves. There was a choice of dishes each morning: fried fish, kidneys, bacon and eggs, and often a blood pudding to please Mr. Richard, who never came to breakfast until Mr. Walter finished. On the cold sideboard, there was always a choice of some kind of game, birds in season, or chicken.

Only one thing was added when Mr. Richard came to breakfast: potted shrimps, a dish of plain, boiled shrimps which were shelled and immediately immersed in a butter and lemon sauce. It was served in an earthenware pot which not only retained the heat but gave the shrimps a distinctive flavor. The potted shrimps had to be on the hot plate whether Mr. Richard ate them or not.

After breakfast we all assisted the gentlemen to their carriages. There were many packages and several brief cases to carry, so Wilson, Thorny, and I attended the morning departures. Not only did they go to the Broad Green station separately but they took following trains into Liverpool. Mr. Walter's carriage left first because he finished breakfast first and preferred to ride leisurely. He did not like to hurry for the 9:10 train nor for any other appointment.

Mr. Richard rather enjoyed haste and it was a bustle every morning when he left to make the 9:30 express. He preferred to get on the train just as it was ready to leave. I often wondered what would have happened if the two gentlemen had met at the station.

Court Hey afforded the Gladstone brothers a most precious commodity—privacy. The house was divided into two distinct parts. Mr. Walter Gladstone occupied the front of the house. He had his own bedroom, bath, and sitting room on the second floor. The beautiful drawing room, the large entrance hall, and inner vestibule on the first floor also belonged to him. His quarters were illuminated by gas jets because he would not have electricity. Moreover, he would not have a telephone. When some important business matter or emergency arose, he walked from his rooms to the servants' hall where he used the wall phone.

This was an instrument with a square, wooden box firmly affixed to the wall. It had a crank to call the operator, and Mr. Walter had a great deal of difficulty with the receiver, which had to be left on the hook while the cranking bell alerted the operator. In his agitation and nervousness, he often removed the receiver while he cranked and shouted to the operator who couldn't hear him. When he finally did "get through" to Liverpool and finished his call, he retreated to his rooms in a state of exhaustion.

His return to his old-fashioned portion of the house was, in a sense, a return to the security of the past. The rooms were exactly the same as they had been when his parents lived in them except for some changes in the coverings on the furniture. Mr. Walter had replaced some of the original fabrics with an exquisite, Delft blue damask. He was very fond of this color and he had done over the entire drawing room in it.

Mr. Richard had more of the pioneer spirit. He was perfectly willing to accept the new improvements, which added so much to his comfort. He had his part of the house, a very large bedroom, dressing room and bath, and sitting room completely remodeled and electrified. He had put in a boiler and installed pipes leading to his bathroom so that he would have a constant supply of hot water. He thought that carrying the hot bath water upstairs from the kitchen in copper cans was primitive and barbaric. Mr. Richard liked to read in bed, and he had an electric push button beside it so he would not have to disturb himself to open the door. This was a most unusual refinement because such electric devices were still new in country houses at that time.

It was Mr. Richard's firm belief that only a woman made a good valet. Miss Poole attended to his clothes, his rooms, and his personal effects. The old nursery was on the second floor in his part of the manor house and it had been kept absolutely unchanged over the years. Miss Poole occupied it and shared a corner with a parrot named "Polly," a great household favorite. There were special stands for this pet: one in the smoking room where he occasionally sat because Mr. Richard was fond of his raucous and risqué remarks, and another in the servants' hall where he perched most of the day. He was such a clever old bird that he was able to mimic Mrs. Swan's manner of speech. When I heard, "Cum heerre, Gourrst, pleeese cum heerre" it took me quite some time to distinguish the copy from the original.

But it was at dinner each evening, when the gentlemen dined together, that their divergent tastes were most apparent. I found it necessary to work out two routines of service. Two soup tureens came to the table; perhaps a thick soup or potage for Mr. Walter, and a thin soup or broth for Mr. Richard. This was followed by two kinds of fish, two kinds of meat or roast, two kinds of salad, and two kinds of dessert. Downes served the wines and he knew which vintage each one wished.

I set up two separate serving tables, so that I would

never serve the wrong dish to either of them. Wilson backed me up with the sauces and vegetables, which were also kept separately.

After the dessert, two different pots of coffee were brought in—one was set before each of the gentlemen. Most evenings they did not converse during the dinner but the coffee sometimes percolated a rather animated discussion, often about the overhead chandelier. This graceless object with eight gas jets profoundly irritated Mr. Richard Gladstone and he waged many a losing campaign to replace it.

"I say, Walter, when will you agree to get rid of that antiquated, preposterous, bilious crown overhead? I can hardly bear to eat while I look at it, and my lungs are filled with noxious fumes! Someday we will both explode!"

"Come, come, now, Richard. You exaggerate the dangers. Mother and Father survived a good many years in the presence of gaslight, and sensible people still prefer it. I think I have made it clear that I would not like to use anything else in the dining room."

"But, Walter, there are not even any shades to soften this ghastly light and disguise those sputtering jets!"

"That *would* be dangerous," Mr. Walter said vehemently, "and for the sake of appearances, I wouldn't clutter up a utilitarian object with silly silk shades. The room would look like a blasted café!"

It was a constantly rekindled discussion, often elaborated, never resolved.

There were never candles nor flowers on the table. One decorative object was a silver pitcher of cold water which stood on a large silver trivet in the center of the table. In all the time that I served the gentlemen, it was never touched because both of them drank only wine. When it was omitted by an oversight, Mr. Walter immediately requested that the pitcher be placed on the table.

"Gorst, I think we all know that water is only supposed to flow under bridges," he said, "but I would like to have the silver pitcher in its accustomed place."

Nothing but heavy, white damask cloths were used on the table. The brothers sat at the opposite ends of the large rectangular table, and the snowy, white cloths almost touched the floor. The only other decorations were two baskets of fresh fruit, served after the dessert.

They were arranged differently by Mr. Downes each evening. The fruit was of the finest quality and came fresh from the greenhouses and orchards every day: nectarines, peaches, pears, apples, and apricots, and choice grapes. The gentlemen never touched the fruit themselves, but every evening after the coffee, I placed a fruit plate before Mr. Richard with four biscuits, or cookies, on it. He added about a half pound of grapes, a peach, and another piece of fruit. The dish was covered with a napkin and he handed it to Mr. Downes.

"All right, Downes, the plate is ready. You may take it up."

This was the signal that dinner was over and the gentlemen left the table. Then Mr. Downes carried the fruit to Miss Poole in the upstairs nursery. We wondered if the fruit was intended for her or for the parrot, but none of us ever knew. Every morning the empty plate was returned to the pantry, and finally I just accepted this mysterious operation as a part of the daily routine.

A long time ago I had discovered that in a household

where the staff worked in close contact, it was better to keep one's council and not scrutinize the foibles of others too minutely and never to discuss them with other servants. Only when the morale of the ménage was affected did I choose to do something about it. The first time it occurred, it unhappily concerned the youngest member of the staff.

Thorny, the little page boy, was a strange lad of about thirteen. I didn't know much about handling difficult young boys but I sensed that his crooked little smile, and his constantly, averted eyes signified more than the fact that he was motherless and poor. I tried to be kind to him, and it was not very long before he adopted me as his protector. He dogged my footsteps, and offered to run errands for me all day long. When I was free in the afternoon, I took him for walks and we visited Mr. Bancroft, the head gardener, who was a fine horticulturalist. Mr. Bancroft had charge of the entire orchid collection and the fruit houses as well.

One morning Mrs. Swan called me into the servants' hall.

"I've sent for ye, Gorst, because I've got something to tell ye that ye won't be likin'. I had five shillin's on my desk which I saw there yesterday afternoon with my own eyes —five of them, laid out in a line like soldiers. And now they're not there. If ye want to know what I think, that young scalliwag, Thorny, has taken them. He swept my room this mornin' and I suppose I was wrong to tempt the lad, but he stole the money as sure as fate."

"Mrs. Swan," I said, "I'm sorry for him. Let's not accuse him of it now. We will leave some marked money in Wilson's room and then we can make certain soon enough."

"Well, Gorst, I'm willin' to see whither he's a deep-dyed

little villain or not—you're the only one that likes him—
which is nice enough of ye, but for my part, the divil can
take him."

I marked some shillings with dots of black ink and left
them on Wilson's bureau. A day later they were gone, and
all the evidence pointed to Thorny, who did the sweeping
in the servants' quarters. I decided to search the boy's room,
and much to my regret, I found the money, together with
a number of almost worthless gold trinkets in a little sack
in his trunk.

After dinner that noon I confronted him with the evidence, and he began to cry. He admitted that he had been
stealing for a long time.

"I never took anything that hurt anybody," he repeated
over and over again.

"I know, Thorny," I said. "You don't mean to harm
anyone but these things don't belong to you, and if you
take other people's property you are committing a crime,
and you can be punished under the law. I have been poor
too, my friend, but I never took money, nor pieces of
jewelry. That is dishonest and you must be truthful in all
things."

I decided that Mr. Walter Gladstone, who, I felt would
be more understanding than his brother, had to know about
the incident, for I did not want to take the responsibility
of turning Thorny over to the authorities myself.

After dinner, I met Mr. Walter in the library and told
him the lad was stealing. Mr. Gladstone wrote a letter to
Thorny's father and asked him to come to Court Hey. I
begged him to be lenient with Thorny because I felt that

he wasn't a bad child. Apparently all his life he had had no supervision and little kindness from anyone.

Mr. Gladstone was most understanding. He made it possible for Thorny to be sent to the School Ship where he would be trained and taught a better code of morals until he was twenty-one. The School Ship was H.M.S. "Akbar," an old man-of-war whose fighting days belonged to the past. It was now tethered to a Liverpool dock and used not to win the battles of Empire, but to correct the faults of backward children. Sometimes, I fear, the latter was more difficult.

After Thorny left, I suggested to Mr. Gladstone that he ring up Miss Massey in Liverpool and get a new page boy. She sent us a fine, upright lad called Herrick. He was ambitious and wanted to be a footman. Herrick pestered the life out of me to let him wait at table. However he soon learned his place, and I taught him that the most he could do, for now, was to learn how to hand Wilson the vegetables correctly. Then I was reminded of my first service at St. Aiden's when, handing the potatoes and cabbage to the waitresses, I had trembled with fear. But not Herrick— he was as brassy as his shiny, livery buttons.

One reason why the Gladstone household ran like clockwork was because it was so well staffed. There were only the two gentlemen to take care of and they only breakfasted and dined at home. During the week there were rarely any guests. On Sundays at least six or eight gentlemen guests came for dinner and the shooting. But during the week, the pace of the activities was moderate.

Off the service court, at the back entrance of the house, were many small buildings used as larders. Each one had a special function. Most of them were built underground, half sunken below the surface of the court. The walls were thick and covered with ivy and Virginia creeper vines. This afforded them the shade and coolness which was needed for storage because we had no other refrigeration. All of the larders were connected by brick paths and little terraces planted with flowers, which made for an artistic arrangement of the kitchen garden and added to the beauty of the landscaping.

In the buttery, the head housemaid churned the butter three times a week. The dairyman brought the milk and poured it into copper pans. When the cream rose to the surface, she poured some of it into the wooden churn, and from the rest the Cheshire cheese was made. She stored the butter in ironstone, covered dishes which were wrapped and placed on shelves near the ground to keep the daily batch cool and fresh. The milk that was left over was fed to the pigs.

The Gladstones raised the finest pigs and breeds of hogs and they even had their own smoke houses. The bacon and the meat, which was butchered from the cattle they kept, was hung in the "meat larder" next to the buttery. But the most unusual of these small, storage houses was the grape house.

Muscat and hardy Concord grapes, imported from America, were grown in the large vineyards. When they were almost ripe, they were picked with a long stem left on each bunch and brought to the grape larder in baskets lined with cotton. The stems were inserted in the necks of old wine bottles partially filled with water. Each bottle was carefully placed on a tilted rack with a special, small platform on which each bunch of grapes rested. The bottles were weighted so that they could not move nor fall.

Every week Mr. Bancroft and one of his assistants would inspect the grapes and refill the bottles with cool water. The grapes would last from six to nine months and there was a continuous supply the year around. This larder was kept in pitch darkness, except when the bottles were filled.

Everything was done in a meticulous and orderly fashion on this estate. Moreover, nothing was ever wasted. When a pig was slaughtered, the blood was saved and brought to the kitchen so that Mrs. Swan could prepare blood pudding, which was one of the Gladstone gentlemen's favorite dishes.

I entered the kitchen one morning to find her standing in front of an enormous bowl filled with the blood of a pig mixed with suet and groats. The groats were oats from which the husks had been removed. They were boiled and allowed to swell, and looked somewhat like oatmeal but of a firmer texture.

Mrs. Swan was wearing an extra white apron and heavy white gloves up to her elbows so that she could keep this rather terrifying-looking mixture under control while she kneaded it in the huge bowl.

I was somewhat overcome when I saw her working with this bloody dough, and I exclaimed without thinking,

"If that isn't the most awful mess!"

"A mess, is it?" Mrs. Swan said angrily. "Ye're too young and stupid to know that I am making a fine dish! Ye'd better sit down and watch me and learn something, and ye'll eat your words when ye eat the puddin'."

Much against my inclinations, I obeyed and watched her

knead the mixture into a solid mass. She filled the hand machine which was like a modern meatgrinder. One turn of the handle pressed out the contents into a funnel-like opening about two inches in diameter. Lying under the opening were the dried intestines of the pig, which had been first carefully scraped and made pliable, in readiness for the filling. The mixture was ground out into the intestine about four or five inches at a time. Mrs. Swan deftly folded the skin over and tied it off.

When she had finished, there was a long chain of blood puddings which resembled a chain of link sausage. They were always broiled and served with bacon. As delectable as blood pudding was to the various members of the household, I never could bear to look at it—let alone eat it!

There were other delicacies prepared by Mrs. Swan which I found much more attractive. The Gladstones were very partial to fish, especially to salmon, sole, and turbot, with a variety of wine and egg sauces. Mr. Downes often said that the Gladstone gentlemen had "fish in their blood." And with great relish he related a bit of the family history to prove it.

Their father, Mr. Robertson Gladstone, was extremely fond of fresh fish. Once a week he drove all the way to the Liverpool fish market in a specially constructed cart. It had a box for the driver and a groom but the passenger's seat had been removed and a large, wooden, copper-lined box had been put in its place to bring back the fish.

Mr. Gladstone fancied himself a shrewd, astute trader and he loved to drive a hard bargain. But the fact of the matter was that when the fishwives saw him coming, the price of fish in every stall went up twenty per cent. Mr.

Gladstone went from one stall to another inquiring the price of turbot and sole, or any fish in season, and he haggled and bargained with them until they took off an amount which suited him.

He bought from 150 to 200 pounds and paid more for it than any other customer who came to the market. But he felt that he had made his purchases thriftily, and no one ever told him that his well-wrapped package was the costliest one to leave the Liverpool fish dock each week.

When the dog cart passed, everyone in the countryside knew that Mr. Robertson Gladstone was returning from Liverpool with "his catch." As soon as he reached Court Hey, all the upper servants and his sons were requisitioned to deliver gifts of fish to his cronies and neighbors. Some was sent to the Earl of Derby, the minister, the doctor, and the gentlemen farmers who had adjoining estates. Mr. Gladstone derived some curious personal satisfaction from his habitual bargaining with the fishwives but he shared his "economical" purchases unsparingly with his friends.

Mr. Gladstone was much respected and well regarded by his neighbors and friends for himself alone. Nevertheless, there was an aura of eminence cast about him by his brother, Mr. William Ewart Gladstone, who was Prime Minister in four Liberal governments from 1868 until 1894. Mr. William's fame and glory added to their name. However, even though all of England and most of the rest of the world acknowledged his accomplishments, his nephews, Walter and Richard, like Tweedledum and Tweedledee, were "contrariwise" in their opinions.

After Sunday dinner, before they retired to the smoking room, the Gladstone gentlemen and their guests often stood in a group looking up at the portrait of the Prime Minister. There was always a discussion of the merits of the painting, and personal judgements were expressed.

One Sunday, Baron Hoffman, a frequent visitor at Court Hey, said,

"It is a remarkable portrait of a very fine character. Surely he was von of de outstanding figures of dis century, and you should be deeply proud of him for being von of de moving spirits in abolishing de slavery for England and de Empire!"

"I *am* very proud of him," Mr. Walter said solemnly. "He was one of the most courageous and disciplined men who ever lived."

"We are aware of your blind and uncompromising esteem for him," Mr. Richard said, "but I am more analytical in my opinions. I consider Uncle William was quite obtuse on many occasions, and his nephew, Walter, is not at all unlike him!"

All the gentlemen laughed at Mr. Richard's remarks because they knew that he was taunting his brother rather than expressing an honest judgment.

The full-length portrait of William Ewart Gladstone dominated the entire far wall of the dining room of Court Hey. The grand figure stood erect with his hands folded on a gold-headed cane. His chiseled features and piercing eyes were outlined against a crest of black hair which flowed backward from a wide forehead. There was power and determination in his face.

The dark clothes with every distinguishing mark—the Gladstone collar with batwing points; the Gladstone tie, a string tie like a ribbon; and the Gladstone boots, high-laced leather shoes—all of the sartorial idiosyncracies which the Prime Minister had made popular, were painted for posterity on the canvas. The grave, austere manner of the "Grand Old Man," with just the faintest glimmer of a smile on his face, made the great statesman almost real enough to walk out of the frame.

The eyes were remarkable and as you looked at the portrait they seemed to follow you from every corner of the room. No matter where you stood—there was that steadfast, half-accusing stare. I caught myself looking at the picture sometimes while I was serving dinner. And I imagined he was saying, "Gorst! Don't stare at me, keep your mind on the service. Always remember to do your duty and don't divide your attention." And I remembered that Mr. Gladstone had never risen to give a speech in the House of Commons without bowing his head in silent prayer. How much I would have liked to have seen him! But he died a year before I came to Court Hey.

It was stimulating to live in the shining reflection of great men and noble deeds, and in my way, I felt that I was the guardian of a bit of history. I took care of the relics and souvenirs of this bright past—and I kept them—literally—polished.

It was curious that in the Gladstone household little of the silver was ever used. Mr. Walter Gladstone despised "clutter" of any kind, and in this instance Mr. Richard seemed to concur. However, it was a matter of indifference to him whether there were flowers in the house, or whether all the magnificent silver ornaments were in use.

But Mr. Walter flew into a rage if he saw any useless decorations. He felt that the orchid collections belonged in the hothouses and when you wanted to see them, you went there. In the same way, the silver collection belonged in the silver vault. And I was the only person who ever saw it, polished it, and enjoyed it.

I had gradually restored the lustre of most of the discolored pieces in the large closet. Only a few more heavy objects, carefully wrapped and boxed, remained to be done. One day I took them down from the top shelf and uncrated them. I found an exquisite silver and gold vase about three feet tall. For many hours I shined and polished the "Gladstone Vase," a legacy of Mr. Robertson Gladstone to his sons, that had been relegated to the top shelf of the vault. If it had been mine, I would have proudly displayed it—a shining reminder of another generation.

The Gladstone family fortune was made in Demerara, a county near Georgetown, in British Guiana, where they held extensive sugar plantations. All of the estates were worked by Negro slaves who lived for the most part in appalling conditions. For many years, Sir John Gladstone, who founded the family fortune, had treated his Negro workers humanely, but he was an outstanding exception. Mr. Robertson Gladstone and his brothers continued their father's policy and actually "freed" their slaves, but this individual decree of freedom was not recognized by the local government, a Council dominated by the planters.

By 1830 the British people were becoming aroused over the issue of slavery. And in that very year, Mr. William Ewart Gladstone, making his maiden speech in the House of Commons, dramatically described how his father had freed his slaves in Demerara. He sat down amid thunderous applause and the issue was solidly before the English people. Slavery was finally abolished on August 7, 1833, and the planters were given twenty million pounds as compensation.

But now there was no one to pick the cane and load the sugar. No ships came into Liverpool and no brown, or "Demerara Sugar" went to the mills to be whitened. Thousands of workers were idle and starving in Liverpool. Mr. Robertson Gladstone was so horrified by their misery that he offered to donate a large sum of money to tide over the workers and mill owners until the plantations could function again. In recognition of his munificent and timely gift, the merchants of Liverpool presented him with a silver and gold vase, a copy of the famous Warwick vase.

When I had polished and shined this beautiful vase, I carefully wrapped it up again and put it back in the crate. I climbed the tall ladder and replaced it on the top shelf of the silver vault. I felt that in my own way I had been allowed to glimpse, to touch for a moment the lustrous past.

CHAPTER

7

Festivities at Court Hey

SUNDAY was the high point of the week at Court Hey. Mr. Walter and Mr. Richard Gladstone entertained at a lavish luncheon for a select company of gentlemen who drove out from Liverpool to spend the day. They were mostly old and intimate friends, such as Baron Hoffman, Mr. Edward Roper, and Mr. George Parr of Parr's Bank in Liverpool. All of the guests were acquainted with the singular way the luncheon was served.

During the entrée and its accompanying wine, the rivalry between the Gladstone brothers became most apparent.

"Baron," Mr. Walter said, "will you have some of my Bernkastler Doktor? I can recommend it highly with the cutlet."

"Baron, wait a moment!" Mr. Richard interposed quickly. "I hardly believe that will please you nearly as much as the duck and some of my excellent, full-bodied Château Laffitte!"

Displaying the finesse of a trained diplomat, Baron

Hoffman circumvented the embarrassment of showing partiality to either brother.

"Chentlemen, Chentlemen, you make it very difficult for me," he would say in his heavy German accent. "I am poseetif dat vatever I have vill be most excellent, but it is impossible to make a choice so I vill have some duck and cutlet, and a little of each vine!"

Mr. Downes poured the wines and the Baron sniffed them approvingly. I served him the cutlet, which he ate with gusto, and as soon as he had finished, he signaled to me to serve the duck.

The other guests usually chose only one dish. But Mrs. Swan was prepared for any eventuality. There was always the possibility that everyone might prefer Mr. Walter's menu to Mr. Richard's, so she prepared enough to serve both menus.

After dinner coffee and brandy were enjoyed in the smoking room, off the front vestibule in Mr. Walter's quarters. It was furnished with comfortable, red-leather wing chairs, small standing humidors, and wine cellarettes of mahogany trimmed with bands of brass. Individual tables with special grooves for the demitasses, port, and brandy glasses stood next to each chair. The room had the atmosphere of an elegant gentlemen's club except for one piece of furniture, a handsome barrel organ, which belonged to Mr. Walter.

The organ was made of exquisite burled walnut with scrolls of inlaid wood. Whatever it might lack in tone was compensated for by its beauty. It operated somewhat like a hurdy-gurdy and had to be pumped by hand. Mr. Walter went directly to the keyboard when he entered the smoking room.

The first time I was needed to assist at this performance, I was summoned from the kitchen. Mr. Walter said, "Gorst, will you please pump while I play?" From then on I was present for all of Mr. Walter's Sunday afternoon renditions of "Sweet and Low"—the only piece he knew. There were just three stops on the instrument, so he set the flute as his accompaniment.

If Mr. Walter had chosen something by Bach or Mozart, or a simple folk tune that was within the range of his voice, the indignity of pumping the organ would have been somewhat mitigated by a charming melody. But to pump away like a farm-hand while a croaking falsetto came out of Mr. Walter's throat was not only an insult to music—it was exhausting.

He always sang "Sweet and Low" five or six times. After he had sung it to his heart's content, he stopped, wiped his brow, and joined the others. The guests never took any notice of the musical interlude. They carried on their conversation, which grew more animated as they drank their brandy, and they neither commented nor applauded when the concert was over. It was a moment which everyone simply had to live through.

At four o'clock the whole company left the house and walked to the meadows and the woods to shoot rooks and rabbits. There were wagers made on the shots and the number of animals bagged. Mr. Richard Gladstone was by far the best shot despite his partially paralyzed right arm.

When the weather was inclement on Sundays, Mr. Richard gave orders early in the morning for the groom and two of the strappers to collect several dozen rats from the stables and put them in portable wire traps preparatory to the afternoon's sport. Then three prize fox terriers were brought out—ready for the race.

The races were staged in a long, narrow passage in the dairy, a cul-de-sac, about a hundred feet long. The strappers would release three rats simultaneously and send a dog after each one. The terriers were quick and lively and pursued the rats in frenzied excitement. The first dog that pounced on its victim and killed it by shaking it to death won the race.

The gentlemen bet on the dogs and usually Mr. Richard won. He knew the running abilities of each animal and by the end of the first race he could tell how fit they were. Mr. Richard was as serious about his dog races as an expert who studies, not only his *Racing Form*, but the thoroughbreds themselves before making a large wager at Epsom Downs. About ten races were run and this sport not only served to while away a rainy afternoon, but also helped to keep down the rat population in the stables and barns.

Only on one occasion were these Sunday customs altered. Then Mrs. Swan ordered the staff to prepare for the arrival of a lady on Saturday morning. She was to occupy the largest guest chambers for the weekend. The rooms had been closed for some time and the housemaids spent most of the week putting them in perfect order. What excitement in the household! It was as though we were anticipating the arrival of Helen of Troy.

This was such a singular event that there was a great deal of speculation in the servants' dining hall. We had heard that the lady was an excellent equestrienne and after spending the weekend with the Gladstone brothers, she intended to return to Liverpool to ride in a horse show.

"I suppose she is one of those horsey women," Mr. Downes said, "you know the kind that rides like a man and after a time gets to look rather like her favorite jumper. Still, I hear that she is the wife of Major Thoights, a very fine gentleman and an old friend of Mr. Walter's. It certainly will be interesting to see how she gets on with Mr. Walter and Mr. Dickey!"

The coachman and the groom went to meet Mrs. Thoights at the Broad Green Station. When the carriage drove up under the porte-cochère, the Gladstones stood on the steps like courtiers ready to greet her. Mr. Downes and I had been ordered to stand in the vestibule, flanked by Wilson and Herrick, who would take her luggage to her suite. Mrs. Swan stood at the stairway waiting to come forward and show the lady upstairs.

Mrs. Thoights was a tall woman, just under six feet. Her bright, red hair was neatly tucked under a small brown, soleil tricorne hat with a snood at the back to keep it exactly in place. Her tan tweed suit was cut like a riding habit, and the full skirt gave her the freedom she required to take her long athletic strides. Her nose was somewhat hooked and seemed more prominent because her face was long and thin and liberally dotted with freckles.

This was not Helen of Troy going upstairs to the guest chambers with Mrs. Swan in attendance—she was perhaps more like one of the stalwart handmaidens of the chase, who knew how to make a dignified and expansive entrance into a strange and unaccustomed temple.

Mrs. Thoights had indeed been given the best guest

suite, a bedroom, sitting room and bath, but there was no running hot water in this part of the house, so the copper cans for her bath had already been carried upstairs from the kitchen and were in readiness for her arrival. One of the housemaids was to act as Mrs. Thoights' personal maid for the duration of her stay.

Mrs. Swan had put several vases and bowls of beautiful orchids in the lady's room, and it was such an extraordinary pleasure to see these rare flowers in the house, that I ventured to ask Mr. Walter if I might decorate the dinner table in Mrs. Thoights' honor.

"No, indeed, Gorst," he said, "no poppycock! We will have our usual table, and kindly put the silver pitcher on the trivet. Be sure the water is very cold as always."

I could hardly keep from laughing because I knew so well that Mr. Walter had never taken a drop from that pitcher and he would never know whether it contained Demerara rum or the waters of the River Lethe!

Mr. Walter ordered tea to be served in the drawing room. Mr. Richard excused himself because he hated tea. Mrs. Swan had outdone herself, and I served the delicate cucumber sandwiches, Scotch scones, and petits fours to Mrs. Thoights with great pride. She asked me to deliver her compliments to the cook, and I enjoyed Mrs. Swan's comment:

"If ye think that puts me in a dither, ye're wr-rong!"

And then, for the first and only time while I served the Gladstone brothers, I rang the dinner gong. It was not necessary to ring it in this house because the gentlemen did not ordinarily dress for dinner. But on this occasion both of the gentlemen dressed to honor the lady. I rang the dressing gong at 6:45, and the dinner gong at 7:30.

They came to the table promptly and Mrs. Thoights looked quite striking in a pink taffeta gown trimmed with matching tulle which unfortunately clashed a little with her carrot-red hair and freckles, but set off to advantage her tall figure and erect carriage.

Mr. Walter and Mr. Richard seemed somewhat disconcerted by the lady's presence and both of them were overwrought and on edge. I knew what an effort they were making to entertain Mrs. Thoights graciously and what a departure this was from the even tenor of their ways. But Mrs. Thoights met the test with flying colors. She seemed to know what to expect, for she turned to me and said in a whisper,

"Gorst, it will be quite all right if you serve me Mr. Walter's dinner and his wines."

My whispered reply, "As you wish, Madam," seemed to ease the tension, because Mr. Richard did not urge the lady to have any of the dishes on his special menu.

Coffee was served as usual in the dining room, but Mrs. Thoights begged to be forgiven because she was somewhat fatigued from her journey. She left to go to her room. When she vanished the evident relief of the Gladstone gentlemen was not very flattering to their guest, but they had the air of having carried off a trying occasion and managing it reasonably well.

Mrs. Thoights tactfully breakfasted in her room on Sunday morning, and after the Sunday dinner she went shooting with the gentlemen. She was an excellent shot.

Wilson, who went along as her loader, remarked to me while we were setting the table for supper,

"Mrs. T. certainly gave Mr. Dickey a run for his money. Maybe now that he knows the lady's aim is deadly, he'll be a wee bit chummier this evening!"

On Monday morning Mrs. Thoights left for the station with Mr. Walter in his carriage. She had given a lavish tip to Mrs. Swan to be distributed among the staff. I had enjoyed the novelty of the lady's visit and I was grateful for her generosity. As I helped her into the carriage and said good-bye, I was tempted to congratulate her on how well she had adapted herself to this bachelor household, but as usual—I kept my opinions to myself.

When the Gladstone brothers dined together that evening there was an unaccustomed playfulness in the atmosphere. They conversed and laughed like two young men suddenly freed from an oppressive burden. Mrs. Thoights' visit was now a thing of the past, and life at Court Hey slipped back into its normal regularity.

Only on one other occasion during the year did the gentlemen entertain ladies. Every Christmas Mr. Walter and Mr. Richard gave an elaborate tea for fifteen of their young cousins and nieces. Promptly at four o'clock they received them formally in the drawing room. The young ladies brought gifts and for an hour these packages were opened with considerable ceremony. The ladies were pretty and elegantly dressed for the party and they chattered, giggled, and laughed happily. It was a welcome change to hear so much gaiety and life in this sedate room.

At five, Mr. Downes announced that tea was served and the guests seemed to dance into the dining room to take their places. There were quantities of tea, sandwiches, Christmas cakes, Scotch bread, scones, and gingerbread cookies in fancy shapes, and it was a pleasure to serve so many healthy girls with such good appetites.

The house was covered with trails of ribbon which ended in a large rosette attached to the napkin at each plate. Mr. Walter and Mr. Richard had spent the morning winding the ribbons. Each long streamer led to a gift hidden in the library, the vestibule, and the Long Hall.

There was a flurry of delight when Mr. Walter announced that the time had come to search for the "pot of gold" at the end of the ribbon rainbow. Then, after the ladies had all discovered their treasures, they returned to the dining room and opened their gifts with cries of pleasure.

Both Mr. Richard and Mr. Walter were experts in old china, and each year they presented their relatives with rare antique pieces for their hope chests and trousseaux. Although they did not enjoy displaying their own *objets d'arts*, it seemed to gratify them to please each lady. The gentlemen kept a file of these Christmas gifts of china, and in some instances, a whole service was being completed—or a tea set begun.

But when the annual party was over and the pretty guests had departed in their carriages, both of the gentlemen retired to their rooms to rest up from the festivities of the afternoon.

This year Mr. Downes and I were in the process of straightening the dining room and collecting all the ribbons and papers, when Mr. Walter unexpectedly came into the room.

"Gorst," he said, "kindly open all the windows wide, both here and in the drawing room, so that the rooms may be properly aired. I find the lingering smell of perfume and heavy sachet most oppressive!"

The cold gusts of air swirled the papers and ribbons into the air as Mr. Downes and I went about our task of cleaning up. But the atmosphere was purified, if somewhat chilly, when the dining room was finally in order, ready to be set up for Mr. Walter's and Mr. Richard's Christmas dinner.

I went to my room to change into my Sunday livery for this gala occasion. This was the first household in which I served where two liveries were required for the dinner service.

During the week I wore a full-dress suit of dark gray wool which had six silver buttons on the coat, three on each side. With it I wore a batwing collar, stiff shirt, and white bow tie.

The Sunday, or weekend livery, was cut exactly like the regular suit but it was made of plum-colored wool and trimmed with gold buttons.

Mr. Downes and I were delighted that we had put on our Sunday liveries, because Mr. Walter and Mr. Richard came to the table dressed for dinner.

Mrs. Swan had prepared a splendid cut of well-hung roast beef for Mr. Walter, a goose stuffed with apples for Mr. Richard, and a celebrated dish which was a tradition of the house, a truffled swan.

Mr. Downes told me that many years ago when William Ewart Gladstone had once dined with Benjamin Disraeli, they had been served with a truffled swan, cooked slowly for many hours so that the meat would be white, firm, and tender. At Court Hey the process was the same. Mrs. Swan spent the entire afternoon preparing the bird.

And when I served it to the gentlemen, they made an exception, for once in their lives. They both helped themselves liberally—neither of them could resist this delicious dish. The dinner ended with mince pies, flaming plum pudding, and coffee served at the table.

As I watched the gentlemen in the flickering gaslight sipping their coffee in the splendor of the old-fashioned dining room—I was standing in my place behind Mr. Walter's chair and Mr. Downes stood in the shadow of Mr. Richard's—I wondered whether they were as content as they appeared. They were finishing their Christmas dinner, just the two of them, seated in their armchairs at either end of the long, white table. They represented the epitome of propriety, but I wondered if such perfection did not contain a certain amount of loneliness as well. I looked at the portrait of William Ewart Gladstone. He, too, had followed a rigid code of social behavior; perhaps it had been handed down in the Gladstone family.

On the day that Mr. William Ewart Gladstone married Catherine Glynn, they walked down a flower-decked path from the church, and later in the afternoon they are said to have read the Bible together at home.

"This daily practice will, I trust, last as long as our joint lives," he announced to his bride.

Mr. Walter and Mr. Richard Gladstone adhered to their own way of life as steadfastly and dedicatedly as their distinguished ancestor.

In some respects, Mr. Walter seemed to belong to

another era. He dressed in a highly individualistic style, in a fashion which he had practically invented himself. For forty years he had had his clothes made by the same tailor who followed his designs to the letter—to the letter of unconformity. For day dress he wore his own version of a swallow-tailed coat made of gray merino wool, which was so dark that it appeared black, except in full light. His vest always matched his coat, and he wore a large black silk cravat and stiff white collar. His hair was black, streaked with gray, so that the general effect of Mr. Walter's appearance was a dark, gray monotone.

His overcoats, of which he had six cut exactly alike, were made in a unique fashion. They were tight-waisted and double-breasted so that the fullness seemed to flare from the waist. The revers were cut wide and the collars were made of velvet for his autumn and winter coats, and for the other seasons, the collars were plain. He always wore a black bowler hat and carried a perfectly furled black umbrella.

One evening I was summoned to Mr. Walter's rooms by Mr. Downes.

"You'd better hurry up to Mr. Walter's," Mr. Downes said. "He's got a lot of clothes up there he's getting rid of and I think he's going to give 'em to you. I can't imagine how you'll look but you might as well give it a try!"

Mr. Walter presented me with an overcoat and two sporting jackets made of soft Scotch tweed.

"And now, Gorst," he said, "we think you should have a holiday. Go into town and visit your family for a week!"

When I left Court Hey to go into Liverpool, I was delighted to be on vacation and I was in good spirits. To

top it off, I wore Mr. Walter Gladstone's overcoat. Harris,
the groom, drove me to the station and his only comment
was, "Aren't you the bloomin' dandy today, Gorst!" However, I attributed this remark to a bit of jealousy and paid
no attention to it.

But when I walked into our home in Liverpool, my
mother looked me up and down exclaiming: "My dear boy,
how nice to see you but—good heavens, Freddy! Are you
playing a joke or are you in earnest?"

Then I realized that something was wrong with my
costume. I had seen the people on the train taking sly looks
at me, but it had not occurred to me that there was anything outlandish about the coat. Mama's laughter deflated
me completely and I decided to give the coat away immediately. It would take more than my admiration for Mr.
Walter Gladstone's taste to carry off such a costume!

From this little incident I learned a valuable lesson. However much a young servant may wish to emulate his
employer, he becomes most vulnerable when he copies him
too closely. It was better that I continue to be just myself,
aspire to be a first-rate footman, and not a humorous
facsimile of Mr. Walter Gladstone dressed in an early
nineteenth-century greatcoat.

As always, when I went home to visit my family, I enjoyed myself thoroughly. My sister Lily had grown into a
pretty and charming woman, but I could see that Mama
and Papa had aged a good deal. I spent most of my time
with them and my brother, William, who had begun his
career as a printer's devil. He now had a small print shop
of his own in Liverpool. I spent part of each day working

with him in the shop, checking out the deliveries and taking the orders.

William and I left early in the afternoon to go out to Everton to take tea with the family. I had one day of fishing with Papa and William, reliving the old days on the Mersey River, and I was glad to see that William's new boat was called "Polly II."

But Papa was not the same man who had sailed the "Polly I." He seemed to have lost his zest and exuberance. The disappointment of losing his business had sapped his strength and he had never quite recovered. Although his hand trembled as he held the tiller, he still looked at me with the same doting love and affection.

One evening I gave a party for my parents and Lily. We dined at the London and Northwestern Hotel, and then I took them to St. George's Music Hall to hear a magnificent song recital by Madame Adelina Patti.

Toward the end of my holiday, I paid my respects to Miss Massey and I was impressed by the size and efficiency of her new offices. She was certainly making a success of her employment business. More than eight years had gone by since I had first come to her from St. Aiden's, and now that she was at the top of her profession, it was gratifying to know that I had been her protégé.

"You seem to turn up like the proverbial penny, Fred," she said. "I have a letter from Lord Howard of Glossop on my desk. He is inquiring for a competent and reliable young man to act as Lady Howard's traveling footman, and as first footman in the *London* household. How would you like to go to London, Fred? It is a great step ahead—

both in salary and opportunity. He is offering seventy-five pounds a year."

"Would I *like* to go?" I said. "I have been living and working for this chance all my life!"

"Good! I will write Lord Howard today and you can finish out the month at Court Hey. Tell Mr. Gladstone that I will have someone to replace you, so you can break him in before you leave."

When I returned to Court Hey, I discussed my leaving with Mr. Walter Gladstone and he was pleased that I had an opportunity to work in London. Mr. Richard didn't take my resignation as well and he asked me why I wanted to make a change at this time. I tried to explain that I wanted to "get on," to succeed in the world, that I did not want to be a country bumpkin all my life.

"All you young men are alike," he said shaking his head. "Never satisfied. This country is going to the dogs—there is such widespread dissatisfaction and disloyalty everywhere and it is undermining our society. You will find nothing better in *London* except more noise and filthy streets."

The day before I left Court Hey, Mr. Bancroft, the head gardener, summoned us all to the hothouse to see a century plant which was about to bloom. It has been said that these agave plants blossom just once every hundred years, but Mr. Bancroft assured us that this was poetic, or "botanical licence," because it would bloom again after thirty or forty years. The long spike laden with half-open yellow blossoms was dramatically spectacular, and we stood before it marveling at its size and beauty. While I gazed at the giant plant, imagining that I could see the flowers opening ever so slowly, Mr. Richard Gladstone came into the hothouse and stood next to me.

"Really a splendid sight," he said quietly. "Undoubtedly the best show we have ever had. Bancroft, in his way, is a genius."

"Indeed he is, Mr. Gladstone," I said.

"You know, Gorst," he continued, "I think I was somewhat harsh with you when I spoke about your leaving us. Naturally, I didn't want you to resign and I thought, if I voiced my disapproval strongly enough, you might possibly reconsider. But I understand your youthful ambitions and desire for adventure. I wish you the very best of luck in London and Mr. Walter will give you an excellent letter of recommendation which you richly deserve."

"I have enjoyed serving you, sir," I said. "And I promise that I will see to it that Paxton, who is taking over for me, is ready to step into my shoes when I leave."

As Mr. Richard Gladstone and I shook hands at the far end of the hothouse, a little apart from the others, I was not unaware that the scene contained a curious kind of symbolism. The agave plant was about to bloom, the nineteenth century was coming to its close, and I was about to begin a new chapter of my life.

Lady Howard's
Traveling Footman

THE train rushed and rattled through the darkened suburbs and I could barely contain my excitement as we neared London. I was in the outskirts of the largest city in the world, and even in the darkness I could make out the rows upon rows of tiny houses alike as peas in a pod.

When I arrived at Paddington Station and saw the line of congested traffic and the crowds of people, I decided, rather than risk losing my way on the omnibus on my first night in London, to take a carriage to 19 Rutland Gate, the residence of Lord and Lady Howard.

We made our way through endless cobblestone streets lined with shops and buildings, and finally came to a residential section where the houses became larger and more imposing.

I told the coachman to drop me at the stable entrance. As I walked into the mews and garden of No. 19, I saw the lights in the service quarters of the Howard mansion.

I was admitted by Mr. Farley, the Howards' butler, who greeted me most pleasantly.

"Good evening, Gorst," he said cheerfully. "How does it seem to be in London? His Lordship told me you were arriving and he has given orders for you to have a room by yourself. It's an uncommon bit of luck. Most of the chaps double up. Come along, now, and I'll show you to the basement."

He led the way down the stairs and we passed the kitchens, pantries, store rooms, wine bins, the servants' dining room, and then, after going through a long corridor, we arrived at the menservants' quarters. I didn't think much of my room, which was small and dimly lighted. Here I was in London, supposedly going up the servants' ladder but actually going down into the basement to live!

"Come up and have some supper, Gorst, when you're ready," Mr. Farley said. "His Lordship asked me to show you into the library at nine o'clock."

In the servants' dining room, Mrs. Moore, the cook, had set out a meal for me. I met Miss Mason, Lady Howard's personal maid; Miss Bangs, the personal maid for the Hon. Muriel Howard, Lord Howard's eldest daughter; Julia, the pretty head housemaid; and the second and third footmen, Trowbridge and Weaver. I could not hide my astonishment when I looked at these two gentlemen—they were both wearing powdered hair! Mr. Farley caught my gaping expression and said quickly,

"Yes, Gorst, you will be required to use the 'violet powder' too!"

After this short announcement of an imminent change

in my appearance, Mr. Farley led me through the house to Lord Howard's library.

Lord Howard was a handsome man of about forty-five. I had somehow not expected to see anyone as young nor as athletic and nonchalantly graceful. He rose and carelessly dropped the book he was reading into the chair.

"Good evening, Gorst, I'm glad you have come to take up your duties. Lady Howard is at present in Italy and she will not be in London for a fortnight. In the meantime, you can learn your way about here and see what London is like. Miss Massey told me that you had never been here before. You will receive seventy-five pounds a year, paid monthly. Farley takes care of paying the staff and the beer money. One more thing, I reimburse you for your traveling expenses. I don't know if Miss Massey mentioned it."

"She did not mention that, my lord," I replied, "but I am most grateful."

Mr. Farley was waiting for me in the large white marble entrance hall. We walked back to the servants' dining room and he offered me a beer, which suggested my first question.

"Mr. Farley," I asked, "what is 'beer money'?"

"Gorst," he replied laughing, "if you are anything like me, that is a most important matter! In all the large London establishments, and some of the great country houses as well, the staff is given a weekly beer allowance. Lord Howard allows us three shillings, sixpence, and you pay for every glass of beer you drink out of that sum. If you drink more, it comes out of your own pocket. We all chip in and buy a barrel of beer at a time—I always see to it that we're a barrel ahead, I might add."

"Then about the liveries, sir?" I asked.

"You footmen wear an undress livery in the morning and full dress livery in the afternoon from two o'clock on. I'll have Trowbridge show you how to powder your hair. You'll get so used to it that you'll feel undressed without it. I'm glad, just the same, that I don't have to go through what you chaps do."

The next morning I had my first lesson in powdering my hair. It began with a shampoo and when I had soaped my hair thoroughly, instead of rinsing the soap away, I left it on my scalp and parted my hair neatly on the side. Then Trowbridge took a big, thick, powder puff and doused my head with the "violet powder" until it formed a pasty coating. After it dried, my head seemed to be covered with a white wig. I found it a bit of a shock to look at myself in the mirror and see how I had aged in ten minutes! Of course the purpose of this headdress was to have all the footmen look as much alike as possible and to create a picture of uniformity when we served together.

My dress livery for the London house was also a novelty. I had never before put on blue plush knee breeches, white stockings, and pumps with silver buckles. I also was expected to wear a claret-colored, swallow-tailed coat with silver buttons, a claret vest, and a stiff, white shirt. All of the staff bought their white bow ties ready-made, which they wore with a round collar. This saved time in dressing.

When I was turned out, I looked at myself in the full-length mirror in the hall—I could not believe my eyes. Somehow I had never thought of myself as a "picturesque figure," but my height plus the Howard livery had achieved an amazing transformation. I felt as though I were going to a masquerade but I hoped in time I would feel more comfortable in my costume.

For a week I had leisure to spend wandering about London. I went to St. Paul's Cathedral to hear the Boys' Choir, and to the Brompton Church where I was often to attend services, and to the British Museum.

One day I ran across a pub in South Audley Street called "The Running Footman," which Trowbridge had recommended as a friendly place. It was almost exclusively patronized by footmen and butlers. Standing next to me at the bar was a most agreeable chap with an attractive smile that showed his fine, even teeth.

"I'm Jim Askew," he said introducing himself, "first footman to Lord Windsor. You're new here, aren't you?" We started to talk and spent the whole evening together, and it was the beginning of a great friendship.

Jim told me that "The Running Footman" was an old pub and that the meaning of its name was even older. A running footman was originally a servant who ran alongside his master's carriage and was a mark of the importance and rank of the traveler. The footman was usually dressed in a black cap, jockey's coat, white linen trousers, and often had a small sword or cutlass concealed on his person, but he always carried a pole about six feet long. This served many purposes: to test the depth of the puddles in the road, to stop the horses if necessary, and even to beat off highwaymen if there was an ambush. As times changed and the roads became less dangerous, the footman no longer ran alongside the carriage; he rode on the back of it.

Then train services began and long trips by carriage became unnecessary. Consequently, more duties had to be found to keep the outdoor footman busy, so he became a member of the inside staff and waited on his master at home. He began to attend the door, the service, and the table. He became a "man in waiting."

Jim not only knew a great deal about the history of "footmanship" but he knew what was going on in London, and he taught me my way around.

I had been at 19 Rutland Gate for two weeks when Lady Howard returned from the Continent. I waited on the steps for her carriage to arrive and, as the minutes went by, it seemed that I had been standing there for hours. When her carriage drove up under the porte-cochère, I hurried out to help her alight. The groom stood next to me, also with his arm extended, but she placed her hand on my sleeve and smiled most graciously.

"Are you my new footman?" she asked. "Lord Howard wrote me that you were here, and I am pleased." I noticed her low, melodious voice and her great personal elegance. She too was much younger than I had expected. I had rarely seen anyone so beautiful.

"Yes, your Ladyship," I said. "I am Gorst. Welcome home."

That evening, when I served dinner for the first time, the family dined alone: Lord and Lady Howard, the Hon. Muriel and the Hon. Bernard Howard, the children of Lord Howard's first marriage. As first footman I served the main dishes, but there was a slight difference in protocol— I stood behind Lady Howard's chair because I was also her personal footman. Trowbridge stood behind Lord Howard.

In the Howards' London house, an entire silver service

was used. When we set the plates before the guests, it was necessary to use a tiny, linen napkin, appropriately called a "thumb napkin." Thus we were always sure that there would be no finger marks on the edges of the magnificent silver plates. I had never used a "thumb napkin" before and I found it rather difficult to set the plates down gracefully. There were still many tricks of my trade to learn!

The Howards were an amazingly handsome family. Although I saw only the back of Lady Howard's head during most of the dinner, I noticed how exquisitely her black hair was coiffed into a high pompadour with two diamond studded combs on the top of her head. She wore a dog collar of pearls almost the color of her skin, and her gown of black velvet with a bustle and long train was most flattering. The Hon. Muriel and the Hon. Bernard resembled their father, their blond hair and rosy complexions made a vivid contrast with Lady Howard's delicate, opalescent skin.

After dinner, the children were excused, and I served the coffee in the drawing room. When I came back to fetch the tray, her Ladyship was playing the violin. She played beautifully, and Lord Howard sat in an armchair enjoying his after-dinner cigar and the music. I had been given the hall duty for the evening and I sat on a tall chair outside of the room attending the door and the bells, which registered in a wall box above me. I was an unseen member of her audience.

A feeling of contentment came over me. Here I was in London wearing the livery of a first footman in the household of an important family. I was listening to Lady Howard playing a tender and plaintive melody. This was one of those rare moments when all things were right with my world. I liked my new position.

At the end of the week, Mr. Farley gave me orders to accompany Lady Howard to Coughton, the country residence in Warwickshire, which Lord and Lady Howard had rented for many years from Sir William Throckmorton.

When the family moved from one house to another, the staff had a great deal of extra work. Mrs. Moore, the cook-housekeeper, Julia and three housemaids, and the stillroom maid left several days before we did.

It was customary for all of the flat silver and some of the table decorations and candelabra to be transported in perfectly fitted cases so that nothing would be bent. It was my job to attend to the silver and have it ready for Mrs. Moore to take along. I breathed a sigh of relief when it left, so I could devote myself to learning the routines of a traveling footman.

Mr. Farley gave me my instructions, which encompassed a wide field and many details. My first duty was to buy the railroad tickets and make a first class reservation for her Ladyship, and a second class one for myself. I carried several robes and steamer rugs to put over her Ladyship's knees and feet in the train because it was a problem to keep warm in the unheated compartment. To insure her complete comfort, I carried a hot-water container to place under her feet.

The most important single object which I was responsible for, besides Lady Howard's valises and hand trunks, was her jewel case. I wore a silver bracelet like a handcuff around my wrist, attached to the case by a heavy steel chain riveted into the hinges. I was careful to keep the chain concealed under my sleeve so that no one would realize that it anchored a king's ransom in jewels.

Mr. Farley had warned me, "Gorst, you may as well know that sometimes her Ladyship takes along pearls and diamonds valued at 100,000 pounds. It would be *worth your life* if anybody tried to pinch that box out of your hands!"

When we left from Paddington Station for Coughton, I carried a tea hamper into her compartment. I was to serve tea en route in case Lady Howard wished it. The hamper contained a sealed teapot with a thick cosey around it, sugar, and a silver bottle filled with cream, a sandwich box, a cup and saucer, a plate, and the proper utensils.

I settled Lady Howard in her compartment, placed the boiling hot-water container under her feet, and covered her with the robes. Whenever the train stopped at a station, I went forward, running alongside of the train, to inquire whether she needed anything.

"Is there something you wish, Your Ladyship?" I asked.

"No, thank you, Gorst. I am quite comfortable. Everything is quite all right," she invariably replied.

When we arrived at last, it was a great help to have the assistance of the coachman of the Coughton staff with all of the luggage. Mr. Farley had telephoned the exact time of our arrival—nothing had been left to chance.

I was relieved when Lady Howard alighted safely from the carriage. This was my first journey as her personal footman and protector and I felt somewhat nervous during my debut. There had been a myriad of details to carry out and oversee, but everything had gone perfectly.

As Lady Howard turned to walk up the broad steps, I noticed a white-haired old man coming down to meet us. He was dressed in a red and white striped satin jacket with an old-fashioned stock tied around his neck, and he was covered with a voluminous black apron that reached to his shoes. Lady Howard shook hands with him.

"Good afternoon, Gulliver. How nice to see you," she said graciously. "You are looking very fit."

"I can say the same, m'lady," and he bowed his head as he acknowledged her greeting.

"Gulliver will attend to the luggage, Gorst," she said to me in a whisper. And as she walked up the steps she continued, "That is our Gulliver who has never traveled. He has been an odd man at Coughton over fifty years and when we rented the house from Sir William Throckmorton, he 'came' with the estate. He is a fixture here, and even if he isn't always alert, he is so kind and devoted that we all love him very much."

Perhaps I should explain that there were always several servants like Gulliver, who represented a curious minority in large households—chaps who were called "odd men," or more ordinarily, "housemen." They were literally those servants who had never thoroughly mastered their tasks, so they had not been able to rise above the most menial positions in the servants' hierarchy. They did the odd jobs, the sweeping, carried the wood, the coal, and the luggage, cleaned out the numerous grates and reset the fires. They were rarely entrusted with a job that required much gray matter.

As Gulliver took Lady Howard's luggage upstairs, I went into the pantry to set up her tray for tea. As soon as

Julia, the head housemaid, saw me, she said, "Get into your proper livery, Gorst, and I'll have everything ready for you when you come back. You have the 'corner footman's room' across the court yard."

I hurried to my quarters, took off my faun-colored top-coat, buckskin gloves, and my tall, plush hat with its little feather cockade. Even though I was in a hurry—habit is a strange thing—I gave that hat a dash of "polish" with my sleeve as I took it off.

Whenever Lady Howard wished to have tea served in the drawing room, I superintended her tray to see that everything was correctly assembled. She had crumpets, plain toast, sliced thin like melba toast, jam and jelly, and a bit of cheese. She always drank a delicate brew of tea made with flowery pekoe and souchong. If Her Ladyship had tea served in her sitting room, I brought the tray to Miss Mason, because no manservant ever entered Lady Howard's rooms. When there were guests, tea was served in the drawing room and it was more in the nature of a high tea, because cakes, sandwiches, chocolate, and coffee were also included.

At Coughton Court, we wore undress livery, so that I did not have to spend time powdering my hair. When I got back to my room I had a while to observe my surroundings. My room was a corner of one of the "U" shaped wings. It served to complete the façade, but behind it there was an enormous corner fireplace in the huge drawing room which made my curious abode a triangle. I was far from the kitchens and the working quarters of the house, so I had to cross the courtyard and go out in all kinds of weather. However, I had a lovely view of the Italian garden and the terraces.

Coughton Court was a beautiful old castle near Alcester, in Warwickshire. Lord and Lady Howard preferred it to their own estate in Glossop, outside Manchester, because the factories which manufactured cotton fabrics had grown to such proportions that they reached almost to the gates of their property. Coughton Court was not very large, as size goes in England, but it was big enough to require a numerous staff.

The house was extremely old and had no private bathrooms. There were conveniences, but only hip baths and tin bathtubs. Gulliver, and two other odd men, were kept busy carrying the hot water to the second and third floors. The bathrooms were placed at the end of long corridors and passageways, most inconveniently located. There were small washstands with cold-water faucets. At least you could have a drink without going down to the pantries.

If you were hardy enough, you could take a cold bath in a tin tub. It not only took some time to fill a hip bath from the icy spigot, but courage to bathe in it. I thought it absurd that such appurtenances as hot water and bathrooms weren't added, but it appeared that Lord Howard preferred the house in its original state.

There was a central tower in the front entrance of Coughton Court which was four stories high. The huge nail-studded doors opened out of the first two floors; the doors had been left as they were in the olden days—to allow the horses and carriages to be driven into the house—now reconstructed into a vestibule. I romanticized all of the scenes of the past, and it was exciting to learn that the

"Gun Powder Plot" originated in this very spot. I wondered if Guy Fawkes himself and his fellow conspirators had entered the great door in 1604 and plotted to blow up the Houses of Parliament and the members of James I's government in the same drawing room, where I habitually set up nothing more lethal than a tea table, or straightened out the pillows on the couches and divans.

Lord and Lady Howard's rooms were on the second floor in the right wing of the house. The entire first floor was the drawing or sitting room which sometimes also served as a ballroom. The other wing of the house was taken up by the children's rooms, servants' quarters, kitchens, and pantries.

The dining room was in the central portion of the house behind the four-storied entrance, and a long picture gallery approached it on both sides of the "U" shaped wings. It was a long way from the kitchens and pantries. Some years later when I served at Windsor Castle, I laughed when I remembered that I had once thought I had walked great distances at Coughton Court.

We had been at Coughton for several days when His Lordship developed a heavy cold and Lady Howard summoned the doctor. It was nothing serious but he confined Lord Howard to his bed so that there would be no complications.

The following afternoon when I was on hall duty, I was startled to hear the knocker on the great doors resound. I opened the doors and a gentleman in an odd gray walking suit and sport's cap stood before me. He was rather small and thin, and I thought he looked either like a jockey or a tradesman.

"Whom do you wish to see?" I asked, drawing myself up to my full height with the secret hope that I could frighten him and he would go on his way and not bother us.

"Uh, Lord Howard, of course," he said hesitantly.

"And who shall I say is calling, sir? Lord Howard is indisposed."

"Oh, indeed—I'm sorry. Just tell him that his cousin is here. I think he will see me anyway. I am the Duke of Norfolk."

"Please come in, Your Grace," I said blushing at my stupid error. "I will announce you to His Lordship. I regret that I did not recognize you."

"That's quite all right," His Grace replied. "My carriage will be along in a moment. I walked in from the gate. Just have the coachman wait."

"Yes, Your Grace," I said and left quickly to announce him.

I profited by this incident and decided that I would never again presume to catalogue people as tradesmen and jockies when they were actually Dukes of the Realm. If I wanted to keep my job, it would be wiser not to make snap judgments about members of the Norfolk family!

But if the servants were sometimes apt to be impulsive, Lord Howard acted with almost exaggerated prudence and deliberation in all matters concerning the household.

His Lordship had even devised an unusual system of choosing his employees. He engaged Irish Catholic women and English Protestant men. Mr. Farley told me that Lord Howard felt this was a most reasonable plan because he had found that Irish menservants were more apt to drink to excess. I don't know how accurate this appraisal was because I have seen just as many English Protestant men-servants quite as drunk as their Irish confrères.

In England, in my day, drinking among the staff was more the rule than the exception. What was good for the master was good for the master's man. Besides, there was a strict code among the servants themselves about drinking, because a "tippler" caused trouble and more work for the rest of us. Most of the menservants who took pride in their jobs drank only beer when they were on duty.

There was a very pleasant relationship among the staff in the Howard household. "His Nibs," as we called Mr. Farley, was not one of us and he kept to himself, even in the evening when work was over. But I became very friendly with Julia Donahue, the head kitchen maid. Julia was an extremely pretty Irish girl with a great sense of humor and a good deal of insight into people, and was a devout Catholic.

"I would almost consider you as a possible beau, Freddy," she said with her great dark eyes twinkling, "if you were about five years older and you'd get yourself converted to a proper religion!"

"Well, Julia," I retorted, "someday I'll be five years older but I'm afraid I'll still be a Protestant."

I enjoyed having my meals with Mrs. Moore, Julia, and Miss Mason, Lady Howard's personal maid. We ate in a small sitting room near the main kitchen, which served both as a dining room and as a gathering place for all of us after our duties were over. One evening, as I joined the ladies, I sensed that I had interrupted a private chat. There was an air of constraint in the room. Mrs. Moore and Miss Mason both looked hopefully at Julia as though she could end their embarrassment by adroitly changing the subject of the conversation. But Julia was full of surprises.

"Fred may as well know what we were talking about—he'll find out for himself soon enough," she said with conviction. "Miss Mason has told us that Lord and Lady Howard have decided to live separately, and that Her Ladyship says this decision will in no way interfere with our jobs and we are not to worry. At times they will occupy the various houses together, and life will go on as usual. They will never be divorced, of course, because both of them are staunch Catholics. This was bound to happen and we've seen it coming, and I suppose it's really none of our business but you can't help being curious. How about it, Mason, you ought to know more than any of us?"

"I cannot say any more than I have already told you," Miss Mason answered discreetly, "and if there is anything in particular that concerns us individually, I think Her Ladyship will tell us herself."

I was shocked by these disclosures but, at the same time, I felt a genuine admiration for Miss Mason's discretion. I did not have long to wonder what effect the new arrangement would have on me. After the weekend, when Bishop Mostyn of North Wales, Lord and Lady Warrender, and several guests of His Lordship's had departed, Lady Howard summoned me to the library.

"Gorst," she said, "I have rented a small villa at Felixstowe at the seashore, and at the end of the week I would like you to make the arrangements for us to leave. Julia, Bridget, and Mason will take the younger children down during the week, and you and I will follow on Friday. I feel the need of a complete rest and a change of scene. The house is rather small and a new governess is coming from London to meet us when we arrive, so I have arranged to have you stay at a small hotel nearby and during the day you will be on duty with us. I do hope, Gorst, that you will take an interest in the children while we are in Suffolk. They need exercise and games."

"I will be happy to do anything I can, Your Ladyship," I said. "And I will be very glad to take the children to the beach or for bicycle rides."

"Thank you, Gorst," Her Ladyship replied. "I will be most appreciative if you spend some time with little Philip. He and Frances, who you know is a most energetic little girl, adore the seashore but they will need a hardy companion to keep up with them."

In what seemed like no time at all, I was frolicking and building castles in the sand with the younger Howard children. Lady Howard did not require any formal meals during the day, so as soon as breakfast was over I took charge of those two small bundles of energy, the Hon. Frances and the Hon. Philip Howard.

At the Bath Hotel, I met a pleasant middle-aged lady, a Miss Bird, whose name suited her to perfection. She was a bird watcher and a botanist. She took quite a fancy to the children and me, and we accompanied her on some of her nature walks. Both of the children were sharp and observant, and they quickly responded to Miss Bird's remarkable knowledge of the shore and ocean birds we saw, and all of the plants she collected which grew in the sand and the marshes. The children became so interested that each one was avid to be the first to find a new specimen. When Philip spotted a long-legged, black and white, wading bird, Miss Bird put her right index finger to her lips, and we all stopped dead in our tracks and remained silent.

"It's an avocet," she said softly. "I have only seen one south of The Wash—the big bay between Norfolk and Lincolnshire. Isn't he a beauty!"

"Is he very rare?" Philip asked.

"Yes, Philip. I would say you were seeing quite a rare bird," Miss Bird replied. And both of the children giggled.

One afternoon, after I had taken the children to the villa and Frances and Philip were having tea with Lady Howard, Julia asked me to wait because Her Ladyship wanted to speak with me before I went back to the hotel to change into my livery for dinner.

Lady Howard smiled at me as I walked out onto the terrace.

"Gorst, I am going to ask you something quite personal and I hope you won't mind. The children have told me that a lady from the Bath Hotel often joins you on your walks. I mention it only because Philip said to me quite seriously, 'Mumie, I am having a fine time here because I go walking with Gorst and his *girl* every day.' And when I asked Philip her name, he said—'Miss Bird.' I am quite puzzled, Gorst. Has he made up this tale or is it true?"

"Your Ladyship," I said, and I could hardly restrain my laughter, "it is all true about Miss Bird except in one respect: she is not 'my girl'!"

"Oh, I see," Lady Howard said and she joined me in a good laugh. "Do bring Miss Bird back to the villa to have tea with us tomorrow, Gorst. I would like to meet her."

So the next day we invited Miss Bird to come back to the villa with us at teatime. Lady Howard had planned it as a kind of picnic on the terrace and she very kindly included me. I served Her Ladyship and the others, and then, without any self-consciousness whatever, she said,

"Gorst, won't you join us? Philip, please help Gorst with his teacup and napkin. He will show you how it's done."

Lady Howard had the poise and tact to make anyone feel at ease and comfortable in her presence. It seemed quite natural for me to be her guest on this occasion.

And so the idyllic days at the seashore passed. Lady Howard was regaining her usual high spirits and her health. She had again begun to practice the violin. She spent much of her time with Miss Hague, the new governess, who was an extremely attractive young woman with a lovely singing voice. When Miss Hague finished her lessons with the children, she and Lady Howard improvised duets for the voice and violin. I never missed one of these rehearsals, always sitting in a chair in the adjoining hall.

At dinner one evening, toward the end of this pleasant month of July, Miss Mason announced:

"I think we will all be going to Scotland soon. Lady Howard received a letter from His Lordship this morning asking that she return to Dorlin House by August fifth, in time for the shooting season. So you'd better be prepared, Gorst, and this time you will have to play shepherd for all ten of us."

Everyone knew that when Miss Mason gave out this kind of information, it was practically official and was invariably confirmed by Lady Howard herself. I attended to all the train reservations, saw to the packing cases, the silver chests, and the luggage, telegraphed Mr. Farley that we were leaving, and waited for his instructions.

He telegraphed back that Lord Howard was leaving London with a private car for himself and his guests, but Lady Howard did not wish to join His Lordship in London. So we entrained for Fort William on the Caledonian Canal in Argyllshire.

We were all sorry that we had to leave the lovely villa in Felixstowe. I felt saddened when the moment of departure actually came because I had never spent any time in my life when the demands of my job had been so immeasurably lightened. Life had been simple and informal, the lovely weather and sea breezes were invigoratingly healthy, and I had made friends with the children. Perhaps sometime in the future there would be such an interlude again.

CHAPTER

9

Dorlin House

WHEN we arrived at Fort William, Mr. Farley met us at the depot. He was wearing his striped trousers, a black sack coat, and the inevitable bowler hat, a costume I had not seen since I had left London.

Mr. Farley was his usual efficient, bustling self and he directed us all into the carriage to take us to Loch Sheil, a drive of about twenty miles. When we arrived at Loch Sheil, the first thing we did was to stand and gaze with admiration at the famous statue of Bonnie Prince Charlie. Then we started for the docks where Lord Howard's yacht, "The Ilona II," was already lying alongside the landing stage. It transported us comfortably to the other end of the Loch.

Once there, we got into the next conveyances, this time a bus-wagon for the servants and a carriage for Lady Howard, the children, and Miss Hague, and we drove the final eight miles to Dorlin House near the village of Acharacle. This was an involved trip with many stops and starts.

It *was* a bit of a nuisance, but there was no other way to reach our destination.

Dorlin House stood like a fortress, an ancient castle-stronghold, in a dominating position overlooking Loch Moidart. The front of the house faced the sea and a sheer mountain rose up behind it like a towering backdrop. It had been in Lord Howard's family for generations, having been originally built by a member of the Norfolk family. This house had been constructed of stones from the surrounding mountains, giving it such a rugged character that it seemed like an integral part of the landscape. There were no gardens, nor had any attempt been made to cultivate the terrain. It retained all its old bleakness and barrenness. This was shooting and fishing country—devoted to the grouse, the stag, and the salmon.

The most important person in the household at Dorlin House was the head gillie, who bore the redoubtable name of Angus MacDonald. His life was devoted to sport. He knew precisely where the best grouse moors were and where the magnificent wild stags hid in the Scottish Highlands. He had a staff of ten loaders and young gillies whom he had trained, and they accompanied Lord Howard and his guests when they went out each day to shoot. Some of Lord Howard's guests brought their own valets who served at times as loaders, although there was a large staff to attend the gentlemen.

When the huntsmen left each morning, we were busy in the kitchens and pantries preparing the silver luncheon boxes which were carried on a strap by each gentleman's loader. We filled the boxes with sandwiches, fruit, chicken, grouse, and plently of Scotch whiskey. There were times when the boxes came back to the pantry untouched, especially if a stag was sighted at lunch time.

All the shooting was done under a rigid code of sportsmanship. If a stag was shot and only wounded, the gentleman had to track it until he was able to make a kill. It was considered a crime to allow a wounded animal to remain at large, and in some cases the chase lasted for most of the day and night.

Not all of the gentlemen guests went shooting; some of them preferred to fish. The Lord Bishop of North Wales, Bishop Mostyn, was a frequent visitor at Coughton and he spent a month each year fishing at Dorlin House. At seven every morning, he would take his silver luncheon box and leave the house, and no one saw him again until dinner time. The entire household knew that he had been casting for a particularly large salmon that had been eluding him for a week. At dinner each evening, everyone inquired about his "King of the Salmon." His reply was invariably the same lament:

"He is still eluding me and I have used every proper salmon fly that I know, and some improper ones which I have tied myself. He just lies on the bottom and looks up at me in his wise, old way. To be sure, I am as old as he is, but only time will tell if I am as wise and patient!"

Finally, the Bishop enticed the fish with a hook full of worms and as luck would have it, the salmon could not resist this tasty morsel and he took the lure and the hook. The Lord Bishop returned to Dorlin House in a state of jubilant elation, and he had himself photographed holding the salmon, which weighed sixty-five pounds. The fish was mounted but the flesh was inedible, because when salmon reach such age and proportions, the flesh becomes almost black.

While the gentlemen hunted, Lady Howard spent most of her time practicing the violin, reading, and walking with the younger children. Miss Hague and I accompanied her on most of these long walks, and it was interesting to learn some of the lore of the Highlands.

Her Ladyship told us that when Lord Howard came into the estate, he decided to have a walk built on the mountains facing Loch Moidart. He thought it would benefit both the hunters and those who derived their pleasures from the scenery. The walk was about ten miles long and well constructed. It had been dug out of the mountains and great boulders had been moved to clear the paths.

In the course of the work, a large collection of weapons had been unearthed. This treasure consisted of many daggers, dirks, and swords made of hand-chased silver. The silver was of a crude consistency but the workmanship was remarkable. His Lordship had to inform the British Government of the find, which came under the "Treasure Trove." This law required that any valuable objects of antiquity found be reported. All objects of historical significance belonged to all the people.

Lord Howard was permitted to keep a few of the dirks and swords. The dirks, polished and restored, were made into letter openers, and the swords were mounted on the walls in Lord Howard's trophy room. The long mountain path forever after was called "The Silver Walk."

There was a huge cave in the mountains along the Silver Walk and Lady Howard related its famous story. Once many years ago, the Clan Ranald and the Clan MacDonald had both tried to rule this part of the Highlands. The cave was the chief secret meeting place of the Clan Ranald. During one of the bitter outbreaks of hostilities, their chieftain summoned them to the cave to lay plans for a surprise attack on their hated enemies, the MacDonalds.

But one of the spies of the MacDonalds saw them going into the cave and he reported his observations to his chieftain, waiting within the protecting walls of Castle Mac-Donald in the middle of Loch Moidart. Sir James MacDonald sent some of his men to corroborate this information and they reported that sentries were guarding the cave and that the clan had assembled.

Here was the opportunity he had been waiting for. He decided to act quickly. The Clan MacDonald approached the cave from the top of the mountain. They sent two clansmen down the precipitous cliffs to murder the sentries, and then the rest of them brought down brush and wood to set a curtain of fire in the mouth of the cave. They kept the fire ignited until all of the Ranalds in the cave died from suffocation.

Dorlin House stood in the center of this disputed territory for which the Ranalds and MacDonalds had fought so bitterly. All that was left of the Castle MacDonald in the middle of Loch Moidart was a picturesque ruin.

Many years before, the lovely young daughter of Sir James MacDonald fell in love with a Ranald chieftain. They were discovered at their trysting place by one of the MacDonald clansmen, and Sir James sentenced his daughter to death. She was forced into a boat and shackled to the sides. The boat was tied to one of the rocks of the jutting promontory within sight of her father's castle, and here she slowly starved to death. Since that unhappy day the rock has been called "Sir James's Daughter."

While I served at Dorlin House there were ancient, clan customs which were still practiced. When the heir to an estate became old enough to handle a gun, he was sent out with the head gillie and a loader to stalk his first stag. No one else was allowed to be present.

So when the time came, the Honorable Bernard Howard went out with only Angus MacDonald and a loader who carried his gun and shot. After the Hon. Bernard brought down an eight-point buck, the two gillies cut open the animal and spattered the warm blood on the young man. By this ceremony he was initiated into the art and tradition of shooting, and symbolically it signified that he had arrived at young manhood.

When the Hon. Bernard returned to Dorlin House with his stag, he was greeted by Lord and Lady Howard, Lord and Lady Warrender, Lord Herries, Bishop Mostyn, the children, and the servants. The whole household rejoiced that he had now become a full-fledged hunter. Champagne was served and many toasts were drunk in his honor.

There was a gala dinner that evening and, after the feast, everyone went to the trophy room to see the head of the stag presented to the young heir. It would be mounted and placed on the wall along with many other "first stags," all identified with small brass plaques giving the name of the hunter, the day, and the year that he came of hunting age.

There were two dogs in the household who were my particular responsibility. The Russian wolfhound, Crofter, was the sweetest and most gentle dog in the world, but the King Charles spaniel, Tobey, was the most mischievous

rogue in Scotland. Crofter always entered the dining room
with the family and he would quietly lie on the floor and
wait until they left to go to the drawing room for coffee.

Tobey would come in whenever he pleased, lie down on
Crofter's stomach, nuzzle himself into a comfortable position, and go to sleep as though the old wolfhound were his
pillow. Crofter never seemed to resent this, and I never
saw him retaliate for any of Tobey's impertinences.

But one day they were playing together on the terrace
and Tobey was snapping at Crofter's slender legs. The old
fellow suddenly picked him up by the scruff of the neck,
walked calmly down the path with Tobey yipping and
squirming, and with great dignity and purpose went
straight into the waters of Loch Moidart. He began to
swim out with that little pest, Tobey, firmly clamped in
his jaws.

Her Ladyship was also witnessing this scene and she
called to me from the terrace.

"Gorst, Gorst—" she cried out excitedly, "please go and
save Tobey! Crofter is going to drown him! Rescue the
poor thing! Hurry!"

I had on my good, undress livery and a brand-new
lemon satin vest with black pin stripes, and I was all ready
to serve luncheon. I didn't much care whether Crofter
drowned Tobey or not, but when Her Ladyship gave an
order, I could not refuse. I waded out to the spot where
Crofter was pushing Tobey under the water.

"Let go, Crofter," I said. "Let go—come on—good dog
—there's a good fellow, *let go!*"

Crofter gave Tobey one last ducking, just as though he
understood perfectly what I was saying but that this last

little act of chastisement was part of his own plan, and it had to be finished. When Crofter released Tobey, I picked them both up and took one under each arm. I wondered whether I looked as grotesque as the dogs did when we emerged from the water. Lady Howard took Tobey from me and I followed her into the house.

"Gorst, please bring some towels and brandy for Tobey," she said. "We can't allow him to die from that icy bath."

I wrapped Tobey in a towel, dried him off, and fed him some brandy which seemed to revive him. Tobey was more chastened and cowed than I'd ever seen him. He seemed to know that Crofter had meant business and only with my help had he managed to survive.

As soon as I had finished my ministrations to Tobey, I did the same thing for myself, except that I had a bit more of the rare old brandy.

Tobey took his lesson quite well, and I never saw him torment Crofter again. His attitude toward the old dog became more respectful. He still went to sleep lying on Crofter's side every day in the dining room, but when Crofter began to growl menacingly, Tobey was on his feet ready to scamper away.

One night a young Scottish priest came to dine at Dorlin House. He had never dined with the family before, so it was quite an occasion for him and he was justifiably nervous. During the main course of the dinner, I handed him a platter on which there were about twenty partridges—a bird for each guest. He took the utensils in his hands and prepared to lift the bird to his plate, but his hands were shaking and he dropped it into his lap. As he tried to pick it up, it fell to the floor.

I whispered to him, "That's quite all right, Father. Take another one—there are many more in the kitchen."

By this time, Tobey, who was ever on the alert for just such opportunities, smelled the bird and seized it from under the priest's chair. He ran out of the dining room with the whole partridge in his jaws. As the family left the table, the young priest turned to me and said,

"God bless you, Gorst, for helping me out. Truly, I have never been through such an ordeal."

Mass was held every morning in the Chapel of Dorlin House. There were always priests and dignitaries of the Church present in the household who conducted the services. The Lord Bishop Mostyn, Father Best, and various other churchmen celebrated the Mass. There was an altar faced in silver, and there were beautifully carved statues of the Virgin and St. Joseph, and a huge silver crucifix. Lord and Lady Howard had two services for the Mass, a gold one which was used by the Bishop and a silver one used by the priests.

I asked for permission to attend Bishop Mostyn's early Mass one Sunday morning. I saw him later that evening, when I served coffee.

"Gorst," he said with a knowing smile on his distinguished face, "you stood out—I might say, towered above the rest. If you ever wish to be converted—you can come to me."

"Thank you, Your Lordship," I said. "I appreciate your kindness but I do not wish to become a convert even though I admire you very much both as a churchman and also," I added, "as an angler."

"I think your esteem for me is based more on the latter

than the former," His Lordship said laughingly. "And from your point of view that is quite understandable."

The atmosphere of Dorlin House was a very religious one. The family attended early Mass almost every day, but both Lord and Lady Howard sometimes returned to the chapel for their own private devotions. The chapel was open for everyone at any time, and the servants were as welcome there as the family and their guests.

I spent much of my leisure with Angus MacDonald and his family. He and his wife had one of the largest and handsomest families I had ever seen. Certainly the largest —they had twenty children. The girls who were still at home were extraordinarily pretty, and the boys working as loaders on the estate were among the outstanding athletes of the Highlands. Angus would not tell his age, but it was safe to speculate that he was almost seventy.

He often went swimming and I felt that if Angus could brave the icy waters of the sea at his age, certainly I should be able to enjoy a plunge. I joined him and two of his sons one afternoon and I swam out a little distance from the shore. Since I was a very indifferent swimmer, I never ventured far out beyond my depth. Then I turned around to see if Angus was behind me. Well, if what I saw was Angus, he certainly had undergone a change! I saw an old man with gray hair and two, long front teeth hanging down over his lower lip. This was definitely not Angus, and my instincts dictated an immediate retreat. As I swam back to the shore, the "old man" dove down into the waters and disappeared. Angus was standing on a rock shaking with laughter when I waded breathlessly out of the water.

He said, "Well, well, Gorst, that old seal gave ye a start,

and ye got back in record time! The seals here do come very close to shore!"

Angus explained they were ordinary brown seals whose pelts made fine rugs and coats, but the fur was not considered very valuable. Evidently at this time they migrated to the northern waters because there were small herds of them off the rocks every day. Later Angus and I saw flocks of gray geese, herons, and gulls that were moving in orderly flights in the opposite direction. They were the harbingers of autumn, and each day I noticed that the air and the breezes from the sea seemed colder and the season was slowly coming to an end.

One night after dinner Lady Howard announced that we too would be leaving Scotland and that the children and Miss Hague would accompany us to the south. Once again I made the arrangements for our journey, and on October twentieth we returned to 19 Rutland Gate to spend the winter in London.

10

19 Rutland Gate

I FITTED the key into the white door of 19 Rutland Gate. I never quite got used to the fact that this tiny, jewel-like key which Lady Howard had entrusted to me would always open the massive lock. As I walked up the vestibule steps, Julia came hurrying towards me and handed me a telegram.

I opened it and read: "Where is Lady Howard's violin? Have outer case but not the instrument. Please advise immediately." Signed: Howard. Then I handed the telegram to Lady Howard. She sat down in one of the tall, petit-point armchairs in the hall reading the communiqué with a strange inscrutable expression. I stood frozen to the marble floor anxiously waiting for her to speak.

"Gorst," she said quietly, "I have the Stradivarius in one of my clothes trunks. I'm sorry if this has caused you a moment's worry. I forgot the outer covering but the violin is in its original case in that valise." And she directed my attention to a familiar clothes trunk which the houseman was lining up with the other pieces of luggage in the Center Hall.

"My lady," I asked, "shall I telegraph His Lordship that the Stradivarius is safe?"

Lady Howard stared directly in front of her for a moment, and I waited for her reply. I noticed that she had grown pale and tense. Her lovely face was contorted in worry.

"I do not intend to answer that telegram," she said almost inaudibly. "It doesn't really matter what Lord Howard thinks. He is welcome to the empty case."

"Just as you wish, my lady," I replied.

I checked off eighteen pieces of Lady Howard's luggage and followed the heavily laden housemen to her rooms where Miss Mason was waiting to receive them. I was still perplexed by Her Ladyship's refusal to answer the telegram. I could not resist asking Miss Mason to explain its significance.

"Look Gorst," she said, "you know what my principle is—hear no evil—see no evil—speak no evil! But I'll tell you this much. The violin was a gift from Lord Howard when they were on their Continental honeymoon. So draw your own conclusions. Thank you for bringing up the valises so promptly." And Miss Mason quietly closed the door to Lady Howard's sitting room.

I wanted to telegraph Lord Howard immediately that the violin was safe, but there was no question where my loyalties belonged. If Lady Howard asked me to wade into the icy waters of Loch Moidart in my best livery or if she ordered me to disregard an important telegram, it was my duty to obey. No employer had ever been as kind to me as she had, and my feeling for her amounted to a kind of worship. I had never served anyone who was held in such esteem by her children, her friends, and her servants. She possessed the rarest kind of sensitivity and intelligence. So I had to have faith that Her Ladyship's decision absolved me from any sin of omission. However, I thought that sometime in the future it was possible that Lord Howard might take out his annoyance on me. I hoped I would be able to handle the situation when the time came.

On my first evening off after we returned to London, I rang up Jim Askew and met him at "The Running Footman." We had a few beers and proceeded to have a remarkably good lobster dinner at a small restaurant in Soho. Then he suggested that we go to the Criterion Theatre to see a new vaudeville bill that had just opened. The headliners were a troupe of German acrobats called "The Flying Pretzels" who did extraordinary stunts with one and two-wheeled, bicycle-like contraptions which they laced to their knees and legs. We were in such good humor at the end of the performance that we decided to top off the evening with a visit to the Earl's Court Exposition Grounds to sample some of the famous American lager beer sold on tap in one of the American exhibits.

I had a wonderful time with Jim, and to be able to enjoy myself with someone my own age was something I had never done before. This evening was only the beginning, because we discovered that we shared a mutual love of music, sightseeing, and plays.

Lady Howard herself was a great devotée of the theatre and she rarely missed on opening night. The evening that "Rupert of Hensau" premiered at the Lyric Theatre, I was on the carriage with the coachman, Derwin, when he took Her Ladyship to the theatre. After leaving her at the door and finding out when the play was expected to be over, Derwin and I went to a public house for a drink. This was, strictly speaking, against the rules. However, we felt that a beer or two would not be too far out of line.

We went into what was called the "private bar," in contradistinction to the "public bar," because we were both in the Howard livery. The bars were really one huge room separated by an ugly, stained-glass screen built onto a wooden partition. Because of my height, I was still visible from my chest to the top of my black silk, high hat to anyone standing on the other side of the screen in the public bar.

The place was practically deserted except for two fish-wives who still had some fish left in their baskets after the day's work. Judging by their odor the fish were aging rapidly. Both Derwin and I tried to recognize what kind they were, and in pursuing this process of identification, I am afraid we stared rather rudely at the ladies and their wares.

One of them caught sight of us and burst out, "Blimey! Will ye get a look at them flunkies!"

This outburst struck us both as humorous, and we began to laugh. Unfortunately, this angered one of the fishwives, and before I knew what was happening, she picked up a fish and threw it over the screen. It hit me on the chest, leaving a large unsightly stain on my faun-colored coat. I looked down and now I could identify it—a miserable cod!

I did everything possible to remove both the stain and

the odor so that I would be presentable when we went back to the theatre to fetch Lady Howard.

We arrived there in good time and I met Her Ladyship as she came out. As I escorted her to the carriage I noticed that she was eyeing me somewhat oddly. And when I helped her to get in, she said, "Gorst, you have a large spot on your coat. Did you have an accident?"

I couldn't very well tell her that I'd been in a public house and that a fishwife had heaved an old cod at me, so I just looked down and regarded the horrid stain as though by looking at it intently enough I might make it vanish.

Then Lady Howard added, "And there is an odor of fish somewhere about, Gorst. Do you notice it?"

"I'm sorry, Your Ladyship," I said, "there *has* been a slight mishap and I will do what I can about it as quickly as possible."

Lady Howard looked completely mystified but she seemed to sense a secret joke, and she began to laugh. I closed the carriage door and took my place on the box with Derwin, glad to be out in the cold, night air with the pleasant autumn breezes wafting away all evidence of *beer* and *fish*.

Once a month during the winter season, Lord and Lady Howard entertained together at a small but formal dinner party. This was an occasion when the protocol of "Backing Them Up" was put into practice. We handed the dishes in the order of their importance and our own rank.

Since there were sixteen guests, there were two roasts served. Mr. Farley, as the butler, handed one roast platter, and I, as first footman, handed the other. Trowbridge was the second footman, so it was his right to hand the sauces and gravies and back me up as soon as the entrée was served. Weaver, the third footman, handed the vegetables. With Mr. Farley taking "the lead," serving only the roast, each footman followed and complemented the others. This was the moment when the technique which we had all spent years perfecting enabled us to serve unobtrusively and automatically.

Since there were two roasts being served, the order of service followed a set pattern. Mr. Farley handed his platter to the lady on Lord Howard's left, then the lady on his right, and then to His Lordship. He proceeded straight down the table on Lord Howard's right. I started by serving Her Ladyship, then the gentleman on her right, the gentleman on her left, and immediately proceeded down the left side of the table. Trowbridge and Weaver backed me up in the same order.

By the time we repassed the course, I took the whole table because Mr. Farley was occupied with the wines, which were entirely in the butler's province.

When there were more than twelve at a dinner party, it was customary for Mr. Farley to have an extra, outside footman engaged for the evening to act as an assistant wine butler. He would help Mr. Farley with the uncorking and sometimes help him serve. But no one but Mr. Farley attended to all of the finer details, such as choosing the wines and seeing that they were served at the proper temperature.

After dinner, the ladies retired to the drawing room, and the gentlemen remained at the table for their port, brandy, and cigars. I served the ladies the coffee and liqueurs, and Mr. Farley and his assistant attended the gentlemen. I particularly enjoyed bringing the shiny silver coffee service into the beautiful drawing room and waiting on the lovely guests individually. Her Ladyship liked to pour the coffee herself, and I handed each lady her demitasse. It was customary for me to pass the liqueurs, and to ask each guest which kind she preferred, cointreau, benedictine, or crême de menthe. Then I waited in the large white entrance hall for the rest of the evening until the guests went home.

Except for occasional dinner parties, Lady Howard lived quietly after her separation from Lord Howard. Most evenings when I finished serving dinner, I chose to take the "hall duty," so that I could spend the evening hearing Her Ladyship and Miss Hague rehearse. Miss Hague and Lady Howard had become warm friends, an inevitable outcome of their mutual interest in music. Miss Hague was a young gentlewoman of a good but impoverished family who, like many others in her situation, had to take a job as a governess. Her voice was beautiful and Lady Howard had sent her to one of the finest coaches in London to continue her training. And because of Her Ladyship's generosity, Miss Hague was eventually to make a career as a singer and concert artist.

The door to the drawing room was always left open. Miss Hague knew that she would find me in my tall chair in the far corner of the hall when the concert was over. She knew how much I enjoyed her singing and it appeared that she gave me credit for a bit of critical ability as well.

"Gorst, how did you enjoy the practicing tonight? How was my voice—any better?" she asked.

"Miss Hague," I replied, "you are improving every week. The high tones were true and perfect, and all I can say is that I wish my future were as bright as yours."

Sometimes my fingers would itch to play the piano, when my duty was simply to take a piece of fine cheese-cloth and dust the ivory keys. I never did touch the piano, even when nobody was about. It was too late to gratify my boyhood wish to learn to play, but being in Lady Howard's household, where I heard so much wonderful music, was to some degree a compensation.

When I wasn't on duty I went out with Jim. We heard organ recitals at Albert Hall, saw the ballet, and went to the music halls to hear the comedians, Dan Leno and Harry Lauder. We also went to Hampton Court to see the public gardens, to Lambeth Palace—the residence of the Archbishop of Canterbury, and one Sunday we took a boat ride up the Thames to Kew Gardens for a "shrimp tea."

Jim introduced me to some of his friends in Her Majesty's Lifeguards who were stationed at Knightsbridge Barracks. I became friendly with some of the men and they invited me, as well as Jim, to their annual ball on February 2nd.

It was a full dress affair and the colorful uniforms, regimental flags, and bunting made a vivid scene. We were seated at small tables for supper after the dancing and a drill exhibition. At eleven o'clock one of the guardsmen proposed a toast to Her Majesty, Queen Victoria. A tankard of whiskey and soda was passed at each table and we all responded.

As I sat down, I had a strange feeling of dizziness and light-headedness. I felt sure that it could not have been the small drink I had just had, but a sensation of uneasiness came over me which persisted until I returned to my room at 19 Rutland Gate.

I found it difficult to sleep, an unusual state of affairs for me. When I awakened in the morning, I felt tired and un-refreshed. Nevertheless, I went about my duties and at noon I prepared to leave to take the dogs for a run in the park.

As I opened the door, a telegraph boy handed me a tele-gram which was addressed to me. It read: "Mother died last night. Come if possible."

Lady Howard was not at home for luncheon, but when she returned I asked for permission to leave for Liverpool. While I was making my arrangements, Her Ladyship sent Trowbridge to buy a flower wreath which was specially wrapped for me to take to my mother's funeral. As I left, she handed me an envelope containing ten pounds. I hardly knew how to express my appreciation. Lady Howard knew how much it would mean to me to take her floral gift with me, because in those days one could not wire flowers nor order them to be delivered in another city.

When I reached home, I had a long talk with my father. My mother had been stricken with a heart attack about eleven o'clock the previous evening.

"When she rallied a little, she spoke of you," my father said. "You were the one she most wanted to see. Then she fell asleep for a while. Toward morning she opened her eyes and smiled, 'I have had a talk with my son, Frederick,' she whispered. 'He is well and happy.' And then she closed her eyes and never awakened."

I stayed in Liverpool with my father and my sister, Lily, for several days. We comforted each other with the thought that my mother had not suffered and that she had gone to sleep like a weary child. I was deeply touched that her last thought and word had been for me.

For many weeks after my mother's death, I attended services at the Brompton Church. On Sunday afternoons I went to hear the sermon given by a young Irish curate. He had a magnificent speaking voice and his warm, sympathetic manner made every word he spoke a solace to me. He recalled his experiences in his parish, which was a poor one, and when he gave the blessing at evensong in his simple, direct way, I had a feeling of spiritual uplift and serenity.

But after I looked at my watch and saw how late it was, I came back to reality with a start because Lady Howard's supper was supposed to be served at 7:45.

When I arrived at Rutland Gate I apologized profusely to Her Ladyship. I told her where I had been, and said that I had been carried away by the inspiring message of the curate's sermon. She listened attentively and said that she would be in London the next weekend and that she would be most pleased if I would accompany her to the Brompton Church. This request rather surprised me because I knew Lady Howard was such a devout Catholic. But naturally I replied that I would be delighted to be at her service.

The following Sunday, Lady Howard gave orders for Trowbridge to serve her supper, and announced that I was to be excused from the evening duties.

When I entered the church with Her Ladyship, I had a momentary feeling of self-consciousness. But once the service began I forgot all about it. Before the altar, rich and poor all worship alike. I have always cherished the memory of accompanying Lady Howard to the Brompton

Church. And I have never forgotten her religious tolerance and humanity.

The next Friday, the entire household went to Coughton Court for the weekend. There were six servants and the younger children to be taken to Paddington Station where we were to meet Lord and Lady Howard. Lord Howard had what we called "train fever"—we all had to be on the platform ready to depart at least three-quarters of an hour before train time. On this particular afternoon, Her Majesty, Queen Victoria, her suite, and her guests were also leaving Paddington Station on the Royal train for Windsor Castle.

I had loaded all the luggage on two large trucks, and the porter assured me that he would be back in plenty of time to get it aboard, but that he had to be at the Royal platform for the departure of Her Majesty before he could attend to us.

"Where is the luggage, Gorst?" Lord Howard asked nervously.

"It's on the trucks, Your Lordship, and the porter will be back shortly," I replied.

"Gorst," he continued, "let's not take any chances of missing our train. You'd better find that porter and have him put the trunks in the compartments immediately."

I found the porter and asked him to come and explain the delay.

"You've got to wait for your luggage because we've got to get the Royals off first," he said.

This irritated Lord Howard and he said, "Look here, my man. Do you know to whom you're speaking?"

"No, sir," said the porter.

"I'm Lord Howard of Glossop," His Lordship said.

The porter looked him up and down and answered impertinently, "I can't help it if you're the Lord Almighty."

This retort infuriated Lord Howard. He instantly ordered me to get the stationmaster, who was having a busy time of it at that moment, but he accompanied me back to the platform. When he was informed of the porter's insolence he asked Lord Howard if he wanted him discharged. We all waited in suspense for Lord Howard's reply, which came after a long pause.

"No, I don't believe that will be necessary—perhaps we are all feeling a bit edgy. There is a good deal of confusion today."

His Lordship's displeasure was easily aroused but he was also quick to recover his self-possession and control.

On Saturday evening Lord and Lady Howard, Lord Bishop Mostyn, and all the children were present at a birthday party for Father Doyle, a fine old priest who occupied a house of his own on the estate. The Howards paid him a stipend, and provided him with a comfortable house and a housekeeper to care for him. We could always tell when he was coming to the Manor House. He walked from his house to Coughton carrying a lantern, so it was possible to watch him slowly approaching at some distance. I waited for him at the door, and he invariably greeted me with the same remark, which never failed to amuse me,

"Sh—sh—Gorst, it's Guy Fawkes coming for dinner. But this time," he added, "for his birthday dinner, which thickens the plot!"

When we returned to London, Mr. Farley announced to the staff that Lord and Lady Howard were planning to give a ball fairly early during the London season, on the twentieth of May. The Howard mansion in Rutland Gate was ideal for entertaining. Its unusually large walled garden was like a small park and beautifully landscaped. The stable walls were covered with vines and formed the background for a raised terrace bordered with clipped hedges. All of the walks led to a central court opening out from the main drawing room, or ballroom, which ran the entire width of the house.

The drawing room was paneled in white and gold, and four huge, crystal chandeliers bathed the canary-yellow, brocade curtains and chair coverings in a brilliant light. The main dining room led into the drawing room, and the small dining room, directly to the right of it, gave on to the large white entrance hall. Each room opened gracefully into the next so that when all of the rooms were in use, a large number of guests could be comfortably accommodated. The circular reception room and the entrance hall were paved in white marble, and here again magnificent crystal chandeliers hung down from the white medallions of the elaborately molded ceiling.

Preparations for the ball were begun several weeks in advance. Mr. Farley and Mrs. Moore, the cook, were in charge of all of the catering and the wines. It was my duty to see that thirty outside footmen who were engaged for the evening would be provided with the Howard livery and placed for their duties. Four of them were stationed at the door, four men took care of the guests' wraps and the cloak room, and the others helped with the service. In great London houses it was customary to have a large supply of extra liveries for receptions and balls, but it was quite a

task to outfit all the extra men with coats and breeches that
fitted properly.

I always asked the agency to send footmen who were at
least five feet ten because the uniforms were tailored for
tall men. When a little, fat fellow arrived, it was almost impossible to dress him without turning out something which
resembled a comic valentine.

A string orchestra was to be engaged for the evening
and Mr. Farley, who knew my musical tastes, turned over
the job to me. At that time Strauss waltzes were in vogue,
the mazurka was still popular, and the polka was becoming the rage. There was no difficulty in hiring a Viennese
orchestra—there were many good ones, but it was not easy
to set the hours because during the season receptions and
balls followed in such rapid succession that the orchestras
had to go from one house to another in horse-drawn buses
to save time between engagements.

On the evening of the ball, the gardens were strung with
Japanese lanterns illuminated by candles which gave a flut-
tering, shadowy effect. The ornate railings of the stone
staircases leading to the gardens were decorated with greens
and masses of white camellias, and the gardens themselves
were at the height of their spring beauty.

The carriages arrived under the porte-cochère and the
guests entered the vestibule where the door footmen received them. A groom of the chambers, a gentleman with
a resonant voice who had been engaged to announce the
guests, called out their names as they entered the Circle
Room, where they were greeted and welcomed by Lord
and Lady Howard.

There were two hundred and fifty guests, and they

moved easily through the commodious, high-ceilinged rooms. The stone benches in the garden were never unoccupied. When they were not dancing, many of the lovely ladies, wearing white gowns or pale, pastel shades which set off their glittering jewels, held court, so to speak, in the garden now bathed in moonlight.

At midnight a buffet supper was served in the dining room; hot dishes such as timbales of lobster Newburgh and breast of pheasant Richelieu, but most of the dishes were cold and served en gelée. The table was laden with delicious cakes and pyramids of fruits and petits fours, and champagne was passed during the entire evening. I might say— the entire night, because dawn was faintly streaking the London skies when the ball was over and the last carriage drove away from 19 Rutland Gate.

Several days after this climactic event, Lady Howard went to the Continent for a week to visit her brother, Major Scott-Kerr. I was left behind in London because she would not need my services. I had a good deal of time to myself and I saw as much of Jim Askew as his duties would permit. One evening we had an appointment for dinner and when he greeted me, he was in a state of the greatest excitement.

"Fred, sit down—and hear the news!" he said bubbling with enthusiasm. "I have seen good old Hales, the Duchess of Portland's traveling footman, and what do you think? He said there are two openings in the Royals and two junior footmen are going to be engaged by the Duke of Portland. How would you like to serve as a Royal footman?"

"I haven't a chance, Askew!" I replied.

"That's a lot of rot, Fred. You're as good as they come. Why don't we both apply? Let's do it together! I'll wager if you phone the steward and ask him for an interview, you'll get one! C'mon—what do you say?"

"Jim," I answered, "I really don't know if I want to leave Lady Howard's employ."

"Now, that part of it I can see," Jim replied. "But you'd better give this some thought because those positions are going to be filled quickly and it isn't every day that you get *such* an opportunity. I'm going to call Mr. Spedding first thing in the morning, and I hope you'll make up your mind to do the same."

For a long time before I went to sleep I thought about this wonderful opportunity in the Royal service. I couldn't decide whether I should apply because I felt that it would be disloyal to leave Lady Howard. On the other hand, I knew that Lady Howard would not wish to deny me the chance to improve my position in life nor to serve at Buckingham Palace. I was so sure that this would be her wish that I felt the conflict was resolved and I went to sleep.

Early in the morning I called the Duke of Portland's steward, Mr. Spedding, and he asked me to report at 10:30 at 3 Grosvenor Square, the residence of His Grace, the Duke of Portland.

When I arrived at the service entrance of the enormous house, I was shown to an anteroom outside of Mr. Spedding's office and told to wait. There were about fifteen other men waiting, none of whom were familiar to me. When Jim Askew walked in and saw me, his face was wreathed in smiles. "Good boy!" he whispered as he sat down on one of the stiff, wooden chairs on the opposite wall. Soon Mr. Spedding opened the door, spied Askew and beckoned him to come in. I waited while Jim had his interview and only a few minutes went by, then the door opened and Mr. Spedding said, "Frederick Gorst, would you come in, please?"

As I entered the office, I saw Askew out of the corner of my eye and he gave me a wink. It could mean only one thing. Askew had met the first test. Mr. Spedding asked me where I had served, how long I had been at Lady Howard's, and how tall I was.

I answered all his questions crisply and to the point. When he asked me if I was six feet, I answered, "Certainly, sir, I have two inches to spare!"

Actually in Askew's case, Mr. Spedding made an exception because Royal footmen were supposed to be *over* six feet.

We talked for a while and finally Mr. Spedding said:

"I think you are both well qualified and I consider you the best of the lot. Wait a moment, please—" and he picked up a telephone. Jim and I talked quietly while he completed his call.

"I'll take you up separately to meet the Duke and Duchess and if you pass this final test, the job is yours. Which one of you wishes to go first?"

"You can go, Fred," Askew said, "and I'll wait my turn."

I followed Mr. Spedding through a maze of corridors to the great Center Hall on the first floor. We stopped before the door of the Duke of Portland's study, and Mr. Spedding knocked.

He entered and said, "This is Frederick John Gorst, Your Grace."

I bowed and said softly, "Your Grace."

The Duke of Portland was about six feet tall, very genial looking, and most aristocratic in bearing. He was about forty-five and he spoke with a slight lisp, which made his voice pleasant and somewhat boyish. The Duchess of Portland entered the room and seated herself in a chair next to him.

As he turned to her, he said, "Do you think he's over six feet?"

"I think he's well over six feet—he's as tall as I am!" she said pleasantly. Her Grace, the Duchess of Portland, was six feet two herself.

"Will you kindly pick up that tray and hand it to me as though there were a card on it?" the Duke commanded.

I took the tray, walked half way across the room, and handed it to His Grace who was seated at the ordinary level. I bent forward slightly so that he could easily take the card from the tray, and said, "Your Grace." And that was all I said.

The Duke turned to the Duchess and said, *sotto voce*, "What do you think?"

"Very graceful," she whispered back quite distinctly.

Then His Grace summoned Mr. Spedding and said, "Frederick Gorst has qualified as far as the Duchess and I are concerned. He can have one of the junior positions when you receive and approve of his recommendations."

I waited in the steward's office while Jim Askew went through a similar ordeal. When Jim and Mr. Spedding returned, it was plain to see that Jim had passed with flying colors, although Mr. Spedding said that he had just "squeaked through" because he was only six feet tall.

"This calls for a glass of beer and some cheese—it's beer time," Mr. Spedding said. "Sorry I can't give you a stronger toast."

As soon as Lady Howard returned to London, I told her that I had been accepted into the Royal service. Any feeling I may have had that it was wrong of me to leave her employ was completely dispelled by her genuine pleasure that I had been able to qualify. She immediately telephoned Mr. Spedding to give me a recommendation, and then wrote a note to the Duke and Duchess of Portland as a reference for my service with her.

His Lordship did not accept my resignation as well as Lady Howard did.

"Gorst, I hear you have given Her Ladyship notice," he said to me in the entrance hall one evening when he came to dinner.

"Yes, my lord. I have given a month's notice."

"I thought you were so devoted to Lady Howard that no position, however well paid and better than your present one, could lure you away," he said sarcastically.

"Your Lordship, I have enjoyed serving Lady Howard," I said as calmly as I could.

"Lady Howard will give you your references, because it is possible that if I were to give a written recommendation I might refer to an incident when you purposely overlooked a most important telegram. Derelict in your duty, I might say—and that might not be to your advantage."

"As you wish, Lord Howard," and I took his hat and stick and deliberately walked out of the vestibule.

I had known that one day my "sin of omission" would be referred to by His Lordship and he had chosen his moment well. If he still held a grudge against me, Her Ladyship more than compensated for it. After I had given notice there wasn't a shade of difference in her kindness and accustomed graciousness toward me. I went with her, the children, Miss Mason, Julia, the new governess, Miss Wells, and settled them all at the villa in Felixstowe. Trowbridge came with us because he was to assume my duties.

I had left positions before, to take the next step up the ladder, but when the time actually came for me to leave Lady Howard, I almost felt that I couldn't do it.

It was Her Ladyship who made it easier for me.

"Gorst," she said, as she handed me an attractively wrapped parcel, "there is a small gift in this box from the children and me. I hope it will give you pleasure, and that sometimes, when you are free, you will come to see us again. I appreciate everything you have done and I wish you the very best of luck."

When I opened the box, I found a beautiful pearl stickpin. I wore it in my black tie each Sunday when I went to the Brompton Church.

11

The Royal Footman

IN JANUARY, 1901, Queen Victoria died, and on the day of the coronation of Their Majesties, King Edward VII and Queen Alexandra, August 9, 1902, the Edwardian Era began. As its rosy dawn merged with the new day, there came a subtle change in the values and social atmosphere of the Court circles and English society.

The stolid, Germanic influences which had existed for sixty-four years during Queen Victoria's reign gradually gave way to the cosmopolitan, international leanings of His Majesty, King Edward VII. He maintained all of the strict ritual, all of the pomp and circumstance of the Victorian era, but there were new variations to the old theme. His Majesty was partial to French culture, wit and gaiety, and he even liked Americans, who were becoming welcome visitors in society and were more frequently received at Court. A period of great elegance, pageantry, and brilliant festivity was about to begin.

His Majesty, King Edward VII, had conferred the title of Master of the Horse on the Duke of Portland, and this

great honor allowed the Duke to use the state carriages
and to have four matched Royal footmen in his household.
We were considered part of the staff of the thirty-six footmen serving at Buckingham Palace because we were constantly on call for Royal functions and paid by the Crown.

My salary as a junior Royal footman was one hundred
pounds a year which was issued to me by the Master of the
Household at Buckingham Palace. The checks which we
received, surely by present-day standards, were extraordinary examples of engraving. They were about 8 x 12
inches. You tore off the lower half, which you exchanged
for your wages, and the top of the check you signed as a
receipt and returned at the Palace office. Actually the check
looked more like a diploma than legal tender.

I was now, so to speak, entering the graduate school of
my profession with the rank of junior Royal footman,
which entitled me to a place at Buckingham Palace when
a vacancy occurred. Thus, the four matched footmen, in
order of seniority: Osborn, Hales, Askew, and I who served
the Duke of Portland, were in readiness to join the Royal
Household as senior footmen at a moment's notice.

Mr. Spedding had ordered me to collect all of my uniforms and liveries at the Sergeant Footman's office in
Buckingham Palace and report at Welbeck Abbey to begin
my duties. By the time I had gathered up my liveries, I had
two steel cases about five feet long, three feet broad, and
two feet high, which contained my full-state and semi-state
uniforms, two leather portmanteaux for my smaller liveries
and personal effects, and six hat boxes.

I left Buckingham Palace in a hurry for King's Cross
Station to make the train for Worksop in Nottinghamshire.

Breathless and heavily laden, I just made the train. I insisted on taking my luggage into the compartment, rather than risk putting my precious valises in the baggage car, because I wanted to open the steel case and look at my full-state uniform again. I could hardly believe that it was mine! I sat there smiling with pleasure and anticipation for sometime, very soon, I would wear the full regalia of a Royal footman.

When the train arrived at Worksop Station, I was met by a motor car which was to take me through the great park to Welbeck Abbey. As we proceeded about a mile into the park, we approached a tunnel. This was the private tunnel which had been constructed by an ancestor of the Duke of Portland. Now it was used purely to save time and avoid the slow curves of the Lady Bolsover Drive, the main avenue of approach to Welbeck.

The tunnel was electrically lighted, which was most unusual in those days, and it was large enough to accommodate a horse and carriage or one motorcar. The gates at the town entrance were guarded by a keeper who lived in the gatehouse. In order that no one could use the tunnel who was not authorized to do so, the switchboard operator at Welbeck Abbey telephoned the gateman when a car was expected, and the time of its arrival, so that the gates would be open and there would be no delay nor any error in identifying it. I was to learn that all of these added devices had been installed because His Grace, the sixth Duke of Portland, did not like to be kept waiting.

A page boy led me to Mr. Spedding's office. He greeted me, gave me my orders, and told Askew, who had already been at Welbeck for several days, to show me the "ropes."

Then the page boy, who assisted me with my luggage, led me to the top floor of the Abbey where I was to share a most comfortable room with Jim Askew. I was delighted to see that we had an open fireplace, which would be cosy in the winter. The rooms were kept spotlessly clean by a housemaid assigned to the footmen's quarters. There was a large bathroom which we all shared. Because we powdered our hair before the wide mirrors and special shelves, it was called "The Powder Room."

When I went down for tea, Jim met me in the Servants' Hall. I was very happy to see him again and even more delighted to learn that we would perform our duties together because the Royal footmen served in pairs. Mr. Spedding ordered Jim to take me to the large living room where the Duke and Duchess were having tea. They shook hands with me and wished me good luck in my job.

I had a few moments to myself after I had unpacked and I wandered about looking at the rooms, marveling at the size and beauty of Welbeck Abbey. After dinner in the Servants' Hall, Jim and I went to the menservants' billiard hall, one of the many underground rooms below the lawn. I discovered it was sacred territory and no ladies were allowed! Here we relaxed and listened to the gossip of the day.

The next morning I reported for duty with Askew. Mr. Spedding knew that working with Jim, I would learn my way about in a day. I soon learned where the pantries were, where all the silver utensils were kept, where the bell boxes were, and last but not least, the geography of this vast establishment. Askew and I served luncheon and dinner together, and my first day in the Royal service went by as smoothly as though the two of us had always functioned as a team.

I spent my first evening on duty in the same room with His Grace, the Duke of Portland. I sat in a comfortable chair behind a twelve-foot screen which blocked off a corner of the room. I could not see the Duke nor could he see me. His Grace disliked ringing a bell for a footman when he wished something, so the man on duty always sat ready within earshot to answer his "hello," which was his way of summoning us. I must say I thought this was a boring assignment, but suddenly the Duchess appeared from behind the screen and handed me several newspapers and magazines.

"Gorst," she said, "move a lamp over to the chair and read if you like. There is no reason not to be at ease. However, be sure not to fall asleep in case His Grace needs you."

I had been on close, or first duty, since 8:30 that morning and when 11:00 came, I was glad to leave His Grace's study and retire.

This was the daily schedule for the lead and follow-up:

1st day......Gorst in lead. On call all day. Serve breakfast, lunch, tea and dinner. Askew backing up Gorst.

2nd day......Askew in lead. Gorst on follow-up duty: backing up Askew.

3rd day......Only on call in case extra guests arrived. Assisting Osborn and Hales if necessary.

4th day......Off duty.

We four Royal footmen never wore the Portland livery. It was our right to wear the Royal livery which we ordinarily donned for duty at Buckingham Palace. Breakfast and luncheon were served in what was called ordinary or "off duty" livery.

Jim and I wore black trousers, a black dress coat and vest of livery cut, Wellington boots which fitted under the trousers and had no laces, a white stiff shirt and a white bow tie.

For tea and dinner, we wore the small scarlet livery and powdered hair. This consisted of a short scarlet coat, a scarlet vest, purple knee breeches, white stockings, black pumps with bows, a white dress shirt, and a square, white bow tie.

We wore the formal luncheon and dinner liveries only when there were guests, and the full-state uniform was used only for state occasions. I soon found that I spent a good part of my time dressing, undressing, and changing my uniforms. And in order to be perfectly groomed, we had to dress and powder our hair thoroughly. It was a time-consuming process.

I discovered to my chagrin that my hair was thinning out at an alarming rate and that the drying effect of wearing powder was going to result in premature, if not total, baldness. So, I experimented with some hair oil as a base before I applied the usual soap and powder. I reported for duty at 2:30 and all went well for about an hour.

But then I felt what seemed like droplets of moisture on my forehead and I rushed to a mirror to see what was happening. By Jove! My "wig" was disintegrating! I rushed to Mr. Spedding's office to be excused from duty in order to make a fresh toilette using the tried, old method of violet powder and soap.

When we served the Duke and Duchess of Portland at dinner, there were always three men in attendance: two footmen and either the wine butler or the groom of the chambers. There was no butler on the staff because Mr. Spedding was the chief steward or major-domo, and unlike smaller establishments, this great house required department heads and assistants. The staff was divided and sub-divided into many categories:

Kitchens and Services

Steward
Wine butler
Under butler
Groom of the chambers
Four Royal footmen
Two steward's room footmen
Master of the Servants' Hall
Two page boys
Head chef
Second chef
Head baker

Second baker
Head kitchen maid
Two under kitchen maids
Vegetable maid
Three scullery maids
Head still room maid
Three still room maids
Hall porter
Two helpers (hall boys)
Kitchen porter
Six odd men

Household and Personal Service

Head housekeeper
Duke's valet
Duchess's personal maid
Lady Victoria's personal maid
Head nursery governess

Tutor
French governess
Schoolroom footman
Nursery footman
Fourteen housemaids

Mechanical Help in the Household

Six engineers (house and electric plant)
Four firemen (electric plant and steam heating plant)

Telephone clerk and assistant
Telegrapher
Three night watchmen

Stable

Head coachman
Second coachman

Ten grooms (assistant coachmen)
Twenty strappers and helpers

Garage

Head chauffeur
Fifteen chauffeurs

Fifteen footmen (two men on
the "box" at all times)
Two washers

Estate Management

Estate manager (Duke of Portland's confidential clerk)

Secretary to the Duke of
Portland

Chapel

Resident Chaplain

Organist

Titchfield Library

Librarian
Clerk

Housemaids (assigned only
for dusting)

Racing Stables

Stud groom

Fifteen assistants

Gardens

Six house gardeners (for subterranean greenhouses and
house decorations)

Thirty to 40 gardeners
Forty to 50 roadmen

Home Farm

Head farmer

Fifteen to 20 men who worked
vegetable gardens and or-
chards

Fire Station

Fire chief   Six helpers (engines, hoses,
                                    water hydrants on estate,
                                    equipment etc., kept in
                                    constant readiness)

Gymnasium

Head instructor   Japanese trainer

Golf Course

Head greensman   Ten helpers

Laundry Cottage

Head laundress   Twelve laundresses

Window Cleaners

Head window cleaner   Two assistants

Such top servants as the Duke's secretary, the estate
manager, the Titchfield librarian, and the steward lived in
separate houses with their own families. All of the farmers,
gardeners, stablemen, and garagemen had their own cottages. They all lived and worked on the estate, which was
said to comprise about 100,000 acres. Thus it easily accommodated this enormous community.

It was impossible to estimate the payroll at Welbeck
Abbey but we were told that, in those days, the Duke of
Portland had an income of many millions of pounds a year
from all the coal mines he owned near Worksop, Northern
Yorkshire, and Nottinghamshire.

The estate of Welbeck Abbey was more like a prin-
cipality than anything else; there were scores of people
working alongside of me whom I did not know and whose

lives had no bearing whatsoever on mine. It was, in a sense, like working for the reigning prince of a small state within a kingdom. Within the borders of Welbeck Abbey, His Grace, the Duke of Portland, wielded an almost feudal, indisputable power.

Position and rank also took precedence in the hierarchy of the servants. They were divided into the "upper servants"—also called the "Upper Ten," and the "lower servants"—referred to as the "Lower Five." We Royal footmen occupied a kind of no-man's-land in between the two categories because we were part of the Palace staff, but technically, in the Portland household, we belonged to the Lower Five.

The two groups did not mix socially, the lines were drawn more strictly perhaps than among those whom we served. Moreover, we ate separately. The Upper Ten took their meals in the steward's dining room and they were waited on by two steward's room footmen.

The Upper Ten had white wine, claret, and beer for luncheon and dinner. The china, silver, and glass which was used to serve them, and which was taken care of exclusively by the steward's room footmen, was much finer than the gentry had in some of the smaller houses in England. Their napkins were rolled up and put into silver napkin rings every day at breakfast, to be used again at luncheon, but at dinner the linens and napkins were always freshly changed.

Mr. Spedding, the wine butler, the underbutler, groom of the chambers, the Duke's valet, the housekeeper, head housemaid, and ladies' maids—and any visiting ladies' maids and valets—were designated the Upper Ten.

At Welbeck, visiting ladies' maids were expected to wear a dress blouse for dinner, and the visiting valets were required to wear smoking jackets (the equivalent of a tuxedo) for late supper. The Upper Ten came to the table similarly dressed and full of their own importance. Their evening meal was in the nature of an intimate dinner party except when there were visiting maids and valets, often as many as forty at one time.

We, the Lower Five, ate our meals in the Servants' Hall, the old refectory of the Abbey. We Royal footmen, belonging to this category, ate at the same table with the housemaids and stillroom maids. The two footmen on duty always carved the roast or the meat, and the hall porter and the hall boys served the meals.

We had two or three fresh vegetables served with the meat and potatoes—all good, solid food which came to the table piping hot and nicely served. We had delicious bread that came directly from the bakery and freshly churned, country butter.

After the main course, the maidservants left the table. Dessert, or the sweet as it was called, was served to the menservants and maidservants separately. The maids had their dessert in their own departments, in the still room or the housemaids' sitting room, where they had a table set up to finish eating. Traditionally the men and women servants were always separated before the end of the meal.

We drank only beer with our meals. Coffee and milk were never served as beverages. Milk was something to put into tea! But beer was drunk in quantity by everyone. The engine room men, firemen, schoolroom footman and nursery footman ate and drank their beer at one table, and still another was occupied by the odd men, who ate by themselves.

Despite jokes and jibes, we took the superiority of the Upper Ten seriously. It was possible to become one of them sometime in the future, and each of us knew that the chance of improving his position was more than a probability in the Portland household because it was His Grace's custom to promote his own servants. Even we footmen, Osborn, Hales, Jim, or I could aspire to be a groom of the chambers, or to specialize in wine and become a wine butler, but it took a good deal of executive ability to assume Mr. Spedding's duties. I don't think anyone coveted his job, because he worked harder than all the rest of the department heads put together.

Another member of the staff who had a great responsibility was the underbutler, Mr. Owens. He was in charge of all the silver and gold service. He alone was in control of the plate closet, which contained enough silver to accommodate hundreds of people at a seated dinner. The silver collection comprised the flat silver service, plates, table decorations, candelabras, decanters, and platters. There was a huge collection of antique Dutch silver, priceless because of its rarity. The antique English silver dated back to the middle seventeenth century—flagons and chalices used in the private chapel of Henry Cavendish, the second Duke of Newcastle, and one gold chalice of unknown origin, which was the finest piece of all, dating back to the early sixteen hundreds.

There was also a complete gold service to serve fifty people; every conceivable utensil was included in the gold collection. When I first saw the plate closet, I was awestruck. I recalled the many hours that I had spent polishing silver, and as my eye took in this incredible and fabulous museum of silver and gold, I did not envy the underbutler his job. He deserved to be among the Upper Ten.

At Welbeck the upper servants adopted an arrogant attitude toward the under servants. Mr. Clancy, the wine butler, was the haughtiest and the most pompous of them all. He went out of his way to make things unpleasant for us and he seemed to lie in wait to detect some small error which we Royal footmen might make. He committed the unforgiveable sin of scolding a culprit before another servant. Corrections were supposed to be made in private, but Mr. Clancy needed an audience. I thought he was jealous of us because we were in the Royal service but Hales, who never let anyone or anything bother him, was of the opinion that Mr. Clancy was just a rotter.

Hales, the Duchess' traveling footman, was an extraordinarily handsome Irishman with a sparkling sense of humor. He was six feet, three and when he was dressed in full livery, he was an impressive figure—and he knew it. He was a chap with a great deal of self-assurance and wry sauciness in his nature and he felt it was right to get away with everything he could. However, when he was on traveling duty with the Duchess, nothing was overlooked and he behaved like a paragon. But at Welbeck, after tea had been served, Hales mysteriously disappeared every day.

We were not supposed to dress for dinner until six-thirty because two pairs of footmen were required to be on duty in the intervening hour, in case there were callers. This left Osborn, Hale's follow up, in charge of the bells, hall duty, and orders by himself. His Grace was very punctilious about an immediate response to a bell.

After tea, one afternoon, the Duke rang for a footman and Osborn did not answer the bell because he thought that Hales was in the Hall on duty. Ten minutes went by and suddenly His Grace appeared in the footmen's pantry.

"Where are all of you—and why haven't you answered the bell?" he demanded.

"I thought Hales was on Hall duty, Your Grace," Osborn apologized, thunderstruck by the sight of His Grace in the footmen's pantry.

"See that you work out your schedules more exactly, so that ten minutes don't go by with an unanswered bell!" the Duke said irately.

"Yes, Your Grace," Osborn answered, blushing as scarlet as his livery.

And with that "yes," Hales was in for a pack of trouble. The three of us cornered him when he finally came down to the pantry at 7:15 ready to serve dinner, looking resplendent and unbelievably handsome in his small scarlet livery.

"And now *Mr.* Hales," Jim said, "where in blazes do you go every afternoon at five-thirty? We're in trouble with the Duke! Do you happen to remember that you are supposed to be on Hall duty sometimes with Osborn?"

Hales pretended to be very abject and feigned a sheepish smile.

"Would you fine fellows really like to know what I do at five-thirty? I take a hot foot bath in a tin pan in my room because my feet hurt!"

We all laughed at this obvious fib because we knew

perfectly well that Hales spent his time with one of the housemaids with whom he indulged in a "bit of spooning" whenever he got the chance.

"All right, Hales," Jim said good-naturedly, "you win —but the next time Osborn is left alone on first duty, I will tell His Grace exactly *where* you are!"

I had been at Welbeck for almost a month when I found myself dillydallying over one of my duties, in the same manner as Hales. When I was on first duty, I had to make sure that the fresh bread and the rolls from the stillroom were ready to be served in the silver bread trays and baskets.

I gradually discovered that one of the stillroom maids, a young lady named Gertrude, was very beautiful, and somehow rolls, breadsticks, and fresh bread became all mixed up with lovely, white teeth and blond, wavy hair in my haunted dreams. She seemed to return my interest and it was not long before Gertrude and I were walking, cycling, and taking outings together on our days off. I decided that I was in love for the first time in my life. There was no other way to explain my unflagging interest in bread, scones, and tea biscuits!

Since my mother's death, I had written to my sister, Lily, about once a week. She was my strongest link with the past and she seemed to have taken my mother's place. She wrote me letters about her new beau, a fine young chap named John Ridley, and I wrote her about the stillroom maid, Gertrude Coffee, with whom I was so deeply infatuated. Lily was delighted to hear that I was in love but she seemed to be amused when I wrote her that Gertrude's father was one of the chief bakers for the Huntley and

Palmer Biscuit Factory. She teased me in one of her letters:

"You have the bakery business in your blood—be careful, Freddy, so that you don't end up as a shortbread!" *

Gertrude lived in the maids' corridor, or long corridor, between the Abbey and the Titchfield Library. This was referred to by all the servants as the "Virgins' Wing." These quarters were presided over by the head housemaid, who, because of her own primness, was dubbed the "head virgin." She was a most straight-laced lady who covered her eyes with her hands in embarrassment when the slightest risqué remark passed among us. We did not dare to use this title to her face but it made the rounds behind her back.

The head housemaid performed one duty outside of her own province. She arranged all of the fruit for the table, and did it most artistically with leaves and ferns. The arrangements consisted mostly of pears, apples, and oranges. It was not customary to eat the raw fruit but it was an accepted fashion to serve it cooked as a sweet, or dessert. We footmen went to her sitting room to pick up the fruit-stands for the table and return them after the meal was over. I'm afraid that we teased her rather mercilessly whenever we had the chance, but I have always suspected that she secretly enjoyed it.

One morning when we came down to our own bailiwick in the footmen's pantry, we found an announcement which we did not like very much. Mr. Spedding had posted a notice in our pantry that Her Grace, the Duchess of Portland, intended to institute a regime of exercise for the four Royal footmen. First she presented each of us with a

* Crisp cake, rich in butter and sugar, containing chopped nuts and fruit.

bicycle and then with a set of golf clubs. We were to spend most of our spare time exercising, and Her Grace arranged for us to use the golf course when the family and guests were not playing.

Jim and I made good use of the bicycles and the golf course but Osborn and Hales were not so athletically inclined. Hales continued to use his "foot bath" and Osborn continued to read his "penny dreadfuls," as lurid fiction was then called.

But the Duchess of Portland was adamant. She decided that all four of us must report for calisthenics at the gymnasium at specified hours and she engaged a Japanese jiu-jitsu expert to train us. Her Grace had made up her mind that we were not to grow fat from drinking beer, and rather than have the beer rations cut, we decided we would do anything to prevent such a catastrophe—even calisthenics!

Four Royal footmen reported for exercise together at 8 o'clock the first Saturday morning when the Duke and Duchess were away for the weekend. The order had come from Mr. Spedding, so even Hales was present. The class was held in the gymnasium, above the fire house, about one mile from the Abbey.

All of us stripped and put on exercise trunks in the dressing rooms. When we entered the gymnasium the Japanese instructor was waiting for us. I will never forget the look of amazement that came over five faces when we regarded each other. Jim was a mere six feet, Osborn and I were six feet, two, and Hales boasted one more inch. The Japanese gentleman was five feet, four.

He started us on the horizontal bars and showed us how

to hold on, and then, with a slight running start, to make a somersault at the end of the dash; I found myself face down on the mat each time I tried this maneuver.

Breathing exercises came next—followed by a vain attempt to touch the floor with our finger tips without bending our knees. Too much fresh bread and beer—we just couldn't make it!

Finally, we were given a little elementary instruction in jiu-jitsu and I was thankful that the mats were thick and well-padded. The little Japanese tossed Hales over his shoulder like a rag doll. David and Goliath!

It was later arranged that we would attend this class twice a week, and the Duchess gave orders that rice was to be substituted on our menu for bread. I was willing to co-operate to any extent, even if Japanese raw fish was to be added to the regime, as long as there was no cut in the amount of beer we were allowed to drink.

All of the beer was furnished by the Duke of Portland. It was kept in the beer cellars adjoining the famous wine cellars of the Abbey, where there was a priceless collection of rare vintages. The delicious beer was delivered from the Worksop Brewery in 56-gallon hogsheads—fifty at a time. The cellars were deep underground and very cool.

Every morning at 11 o'clock, the Master of the Servants' Hall brought a two-gallon, copper pitcher of beer to the footmen's pantry, together with some fine, crusty bread and Cheshire cheese. Beer was again served at the midday meal, and at seven we had several glasses, and at 9:00 o'clock supper, the copper pitcher reappeared foaming, full. I suppose the Duchess was justified in trying to insure the slim appearance and erect posture of her Royal footmen, who were more partial to beer than to exercise.

But the Duchess' interest in her household was not confined to food and drink. Early one Sunday morning we were straightening up the Gothic Hall, when Her Grace entered and went to the piano. Although Jim and I had not finished we made a gesture to withdraw, and we looked at the Duchess for her tacit instruction. She turned to us but instead of the expected, "You may go," she said, very charmingly,

"Gorst and Askew, won't you come to the piano and join me in singing a hymn?"

Jim looked at me as though he had been hit by a bolt of lightning, but I thought this was an amusing situation and I determined to give it my best efforts. I sang loudly and dedicatedly—how musically I don't know—and Askew tried to keep up with me. This he did with grimaces and raised eyebrows, a desperate signal for me to tone down my voice from a forte to a less taxing pianissimo. But I was having too good a time watching Jim squirm and I went on singing lustily. Her Grace was so pleased by our rendition that she issued us another invitation immediately.

"Gorst and Askew," she said, "that was splendid. You have been so very obliging that I would like you both to join me and the children and the rest of the family at morning prayers at 11 o'clock. I want you to sing just as loudly as you can for the Duke."

When we left the drawing room, Askew was red in the face and it did not take long for me to know the reason why.

"You really are the choir boy!" he said. "You like to sing but I don't. I can hardly carry a tune! How am I going to get out of this? We'll be the butt of every joke in the billiard room!"

"Jim," I said, "you're not going to get out of it. Resign yourself and try to stay on key."

Askew reported with me for prayers and we repeated the performance. Her Grace was pleased, but I wondered if any of the footmen had heard or seen us sing. As much as I enjoyed it, I too did not wish to be the subject of a crude "joke." But nothing was ever mentioned about our musical rendition by Osborn or Hales.

We had sung the praises of the Lord, and He had protected us from the Philistines in the billiard room.

Welbeck Abbey

IN THE twelfth century a group of monks, the Premonstratensians, so called because they wore white habits, had about thirty-five houses for their members in England. There are still remains of some of them: Easby, Bayham, Yorkshire, and Welbeck Abbey.

Welbeck Abbey was founded by Thomas de Cuckney, and was the head house of the Order until Henry VIII ordered the confiscation and dissolution of the monasteries. It was surrendered on June 20, 1538.

While I served at Welbeck Abbey, I was reminded every day of its imposing splendor and its venerable connection with the last seven centuries. Not very much of the original Abbey remained, except the arches forming part of the cellar in the servants' quarters. But for more than three hundred years the various owners of Welbeck Abbey had added to it. The most extensive and imaginative additions were made by the fifth Duke of Portland.

William John Cavendish Bentinck, the fifth Duke of

Portland, was born on September 18, 1800. His Grace never married and was considered a recluse. However, it was said that he was as happy as a man could be when he was engaged in some vast building program, and he was adored by the architects and workmen with whom he spent most of his life. For 18 years he literally transformed the estate into one large workshop, and he employed as many as 15,000 men to carry out his plans. The annual bill for his continuous additions was over £100,000 a year. While his enormous projects were in progress, he lived in a suite of four rooms and his only contact with the outside world was through two letter boxes for his mail: one marked "incoming" and the other "outgoing."

These eccentricities may explain why most of his additions were built underground, subterranean rooms below the lawns. However, these rooms were not dark. They were completely lighted by domed skylights camouflaged in the lawn above and by thousands of gas jets inside. The vast ballroom, which was also used as a picture gallery, was 160 feet long and 63 feet wide and it was the largest room in England ever built without the support of pillars.

While I was at Welbeck, a series of wonderful portraits of the relatives of the Portland family graced the ballroom walls, among them the remarkable likenesses of the Earls of Southampton, and a beautiful drawing of an angel by Sir Joshua Reynolds which he had given to the third Duke of Portland. There were numerous other rooms in this subterranean mansion: reception rooms, kitchens, pantries, a library, and many other similar chambers connected to other parts of the house by tunnels.

The principal tunnel, connecting the kitchen wing to

the main portion of the house, was laid with trolley lines so that large trucks, all fitted with rubber wheels, could move noiselessly along the tracks and carry the food as quickly as possible to the main dining room. The trucks were fitted with plates heated by hot water on one side to keep the dishes hot, and on the other there were cold steel plates for chilled food. The underground trolley was kept in perfect condition and it was always a source of great interest to the many visitors who came to Welbeck.

One building which the fifth Duke of Portland built above the ground was the famous New Riding School. The School was approximately 400 feet long, 106 feet wide and over 50 feet high. It was built of stone and it had no windows, but it was perfectly lighted by the vaulted ceiling of glass that rested on a cast iron support. The center of the ceiling was decorated with a frieze of foliage, animals, and birds. The School is still regarded as one of the greatest achievements in cast iron architecture, and contained the second largest enclosed riding ring in the world. The largest one, built by the Tsars, was in Moscow.

In 1879, the fifth Duke of Portland died, and some time afterward the title came to the sixth Duke of Portland, Sir William John Arthur Charles James Cavendish-Bentinck, whom it was my privilege to serve.

His Grace was born on December 28, 1857. He married Her Grace, the Duchess of Portland, on June 11, 1889. She was Winifred Anna, the daughter of Thomas Yorke of Walmsgate. The Duke and Duchess of Portland held two of the highest honorary positions granted by His Majesty, King Edward VII: His Grace was appointed Master of the Horse, and later Her Grace became the

Mistress of the Robes to Her Majesty, Queen Alexandra, following the Duchess of Buccleuch who had been accorded this honor by Queen Victoria.

The Duke and Duchess had three great houses: 3 Grosvenor Square in London, Langwell in County Caithness, Scotland, and their favorite residence, Welbeck Abbey in Nottinghamshire.

The Duke may not have been as great a builder as his predecessor but he maintained the estate with meticulous devotion, particularly improving the racing stables. He loved the raising and breeding of horses, and his stables were among the finest in England. In one year his horses won the Oaks, the Ascot Gold Cup, and the Derby. He gave some of the prize to the Duchess and she had a row of cottages built called "The Winnings," which were given to old, retired couples who had worked on the estate. These elderly retainers kept their cottages and grounds in beautiful order, vying with each other every year to win a prize for the prettiest garden.

Occasionally I had the opportunity to go to the stables to see the Duke's thoroughbreds but, for the most part, I was confined to the Abbey, a castle of unparalleled magnificence and solidity.

The entrance hall to Welbeck was spacious and paneled in oak, and hung with tapestries. It was sparsely and formally furnished with tall chairs and several large tables, with many individual pieces of fine porcelain on display. But one handsome *objet d'art* immediately attracted one's attention—a portrait bust of Kaiser Wilhelm II, sculptured in white marble.

It dominated the room from its matching pedestal. The

artist had carved every detail with infinite care, and even the characteristic ascending, square mustache, and the medals on Kaiser Wilhelm II's field marshal's uniform were easily distinguishable from the far side of the hall. He had been a guest at Welbeck, and he must have thought that this solid memento of his visit, which he presented to the Duke of Portland, would allow him to survey the grand entrance hall for all time to come.

The entrance hall merged into the Gothic Hall, recently restored after a devastating fire destroyed the original one built in 1715 by Lady Margaret Cavendish. Lady Margaret had owned Welbeck and brought it to the Bentinck family when she married the second Duke of Portland.

The present Gothic Hall, the sitting room, was four stories high and rose majestically to the ceiling, a series of graceful Gothic vaults. A silver lantern hung down from the apex of each arch, adding a light and ethereal touch to the splendor. An enormous fireplace of stone and marble, emblazoned with the Portland coat of arms, dominated the room. As one approached it, one saw the words "Craignez Honte," (Fear Dishonor) the motto of the Portland family.

At the far end of the Gothic Hall, five steps rose to a mounted dais. A magnificent piano (chosen for Her Grace by Paderewski) shared this place of esteem with a rare silver cistern which had served in the early days of silver tableware as a convenient vessel in which to wash the silver in the dining room as it was used. This solid silver object, of the period of Charles II, weighed 1160 ounces and stood on feet in the shape of lions' paws.

Next to the sitting room was the State Drawing Room. The rugs, walls, and furniture were all made of tapestry of the same design. Other notable features of the room were the gold and mirror overmantel, the display of gold and jeweled snuff boxes, and the priceless collection of miniatures.

Among the other family heirlooms exhibited were a ruby ring which William of Orange gave to Queen Mary to wear at their coronation, the seal of King Charles I carved into an emerald, the pearl earring worn by Charles Stuart when he was beheaded, and a dagger which had belonged to Henry VIII.

Three huge crystal chandeliers shimmered like diamonds on the ceiling, and bathed the room with their faceted reflections. A corridor led to the Blue Library, which contained a large number of manuscripts and books but not nearly the number which crowded the Titchfield Library. At the end of the corridor was a marble loggia, filled with flowering plants, which gave onto the terrace when the great doors were opened.

The Duchess's apartment also overlooked the terrace. Her Grace's sitting room was furnished with exquisite, inlaid French furniture. The panels in the gilt and white walls and the chairs were covered in electric blue brocade. Her Grace's bedroom and dressing room were paneled in ivory-white silk damask with the voluminous curtains and furniture coverings done in the same material. The toilet accessories were rock crystal with her coat of arms inlaid in gold.

The bed had a huge canopy of the ivory-white damask which draped from the peak of the ornamental gilt coronet to the floor. Her Grace's bathroom was made entirely of green marble, and four steps descended to the bath, which had bronze lions' heads for faucets.

Next to the Duchess's suite was the State Apartment, closed off from the Grand Corridor by heavy grilled doors. This apartment consisted of a drawing room, lady's dressing room, bedroom, gentleman's dressing room, two bathrooms, two rooms for a gentleman and a lady in waiting, and a large foyer. The whole apartment was paneled and furnished in blue brocade with rugs of the same color. The apartment was used only by Royal guests or distinguished visitors.

The grand staircase, built of polished oak, went from the basement to the fifth floor. The third and fourth floors of the Abbey were entirely devoted to seemingly endless corridors of guests' rooms, except for the nursery and school room apartments on the third floor, directly over the State Apartment. The fifth floor was occupied only by the servants, who had a long, long climb to their rooms.

The kitchen was a separate building opposite the Chapel and the Titchfield Library. The buildings were divided by a charming courtyard and garden which extended to the back of the Abbey. The building which housed the kitchen also had many other rooms. There was a large scullery where all the pots and pans were washed and scoured, a vegetable room, auxiliary kitchen, servants' sitting room, larders, pickling room, stillroom, and the bakery where all the bread and rolls were made. The visiting servants' rooms and baths took up the other wing, which could easily accommodate forty people.

The kitchen itself was four stories high and about eighty feet square. A large open fireplace, about fifteen feet wide, occupied the center wall and here all the roasting was done on suspended spits. It took about two hundred pounds of coal every day to set the fire going properly and keep it in good cooking condition. A semicircular iron screen, fitted with compartments to heat the serving dishes, stood at one side of the fireplace.

All the other cooking was done on iron gas ranges and steam-heated hot plates were in constant use for dishing up the food. There were racks and shelves on the sides of the tunnel which led to the main dining room so that all the serving dishes could be quickly arranged on the trolleys as they left for the main house.

There were two dining rooms in the Abbey, one more formal than the other, called the "State Dining Room," and in them hung paintings by Rembrandt, Van Dyck, and Lily. On state occasions both were used but when the Duke and Duchess dined alone, they used the "Small Dining Room."

And at the end of the dining room wing was an exquisite drawing room called the "Swan Room." This salon, entirely furnished in eighteenth-century French furniture, was named for the Aubusson rug which decorated the floor. Marie Antoinette had presented it to one of the Duchesses of Portland and it depicted two swans facing each other, holding a wide pink ribbon which flowed through their beaks into the design of the flowered border.

The dining room and the "Swan Room" faced the large terrace which looked out over a lake. In spring, this beautiful terrace was furnished with handmade wicker chairs and settees covered in gay chintz, and tables that held brightly colored sunshades. It was here, on sunny afternoons, that

Her Grace, the Duchess of Portland, served tea to her many distinguished guests.

The crowning glory of Welbeck was the Titchfield Library. It occupied more than half of the Chapel building, which was four stories high. One of the Duke of Portland's ancestors had engaged a mural painter to decorate the ceiling of the library with his impression of the aurora borealis.

His Grace disliked this painting so heartily that he had a false ceiling built which blocked out the omnipresent copy of the northern lights and made the height of the rotunda two stories less. Still His Grace was considerate enough to build a gallery above the false ceiling, so that those who wished could look at his ancestor's celestial caprice.

Some years later, when I saw the interior of the Graf Zeppelin, I was reminded of my walk around the gallery of the Titchfield Library. I saw the sky above me and the framework below and I again felt as though I were walking on air.

The building contained a vast collection of manuscripts, incunabula, and letters. Among them was the famous collection of letters written to William Bentinck, the first Earl of Portland, by King William III in his own hand.

The gardens of Welbeck were beautiful almost beyond description, and there were also orangeries, vineries, and tropical conservatories, an apricot house, and the most extensive hothouses in England. One hothouse contained only rare Indian and African fruits, and still another was exclusively devoted to the culture of carnations, the Duchess of Portland's favorite flower. The great Park included stately beeches and hoary oaks (the most famous of them, the Greendale Oak with an archway cut through its trunk in 1724), three lakes, and an eighteen hole golf course.

The county agricultural shows and cricket matches were held on the property and thousands of people attended. When they left, the roadways, gravel paths, and lawns were instantly raked and swept.

To look at Welbeck from a distance in the sunlight, was like looking toward the castle described in every fairy tale. The tower where the Duke's banners were displayed, the soft green of the copper roof, the balustrades and terraces, all set off by the rose gardens and vivid flower borders, and the swans gliding over the lakes, created a scene which only a great poet could describe.

Early one autumn morning, a flock of wild Canada geese came down into the midst of all of this ordered grandeur and established elegance. They were identified as migratory visitors from the far shores of North America. There was a good deal of interest because they were considered fairly rare, and the Duchess of Portland, who loved birds and headed the Royal Society for their protection, gave orders that grain should be put out and that no one was to molest them.

The creatures must have sensed that they were welcome guests, and they settled down at the lake and stayed for the winter. In spring they left, probably to fly across the sea to their ancestral breeding grounds. But the following autumn they returned. Perhaps they knew instinctively that at Welbeck they would find sanctuary and the bountiful grain of the Duchess of Portland.

13

The Servants' Ball

FREQUENTLY the day began very early for Askew and me. Some mornings we arose at five o'clock so that we could go with the coachman when he exercised the "greys," the magnificent white horses which were bred on the estate. Kaiser Wilhelm had presented the first pair to the Duke of Portland and now there were eight of these wonderful animals in the stables.

We harnessed a pair to a carriage and drove about ten miles at a steady pace just to keep them in trim. We sat with the coachman for this early-morning run, almost always within the grounds and confines of Welbeck. Occasionally when we went to Worksop, we stopped at the inn and had a rum and milk before breakfast, and we always stood treat for Fisher, the coachman. He was a little fellow who knew more about horses than most great, professional trainers, and became head coachman for the Duke some years later.

When we returned, we prepared to serve breakfast to

the guests who came down to the dining room. When there were large shooting parties during the autumn, the gentlemen ate at the table but most of the ladies breakfasted in their rooms. Even if there were twenty or thirty guests, the housemaids carried up the ladies' trays, and the footmen on first duty served from the sideboards and hot plates in the dining room.

The Duke of Portland and his shooting companions, often including the Duke of Devonshire, the Duke of Marlborough, the Duke of Sutherland, Count Apponyi, and many others, would leave the house in the morning to shoot in the preserves which were originally part of the old Sherwood Forest. They met at Robin Hood's Larder for luncheon after they had bagged hundreds of partridges and pheasants, and here the ladies joined them for what might be called an elaborate picnic. The ladies came by carriage, all wearing tailored costumes, and what today we would call "sensible shoes."

The supplies, which were brought to Robin Hood's Larder by lorry, included chilled wine and an individual partridge or a portion of pheasant for each guest. On one occasion, when Jim and I were on first duty, a delegation from the miners, who were on strike in one of the Duke's Worksop coal mines, interrupted the luncheon and demanded to see the Duke himself.

I summoned His Grace and we listened tensely while the miners' spokesman demanded something to eat because they were starving. The hungry miners and the Duke of Portland facing and glaring at each other boded violence.

But in front of his uneasy guests His Grace handled the explosive situation with tact and diplomacy. He ordered

us to get the partridges that had been bagged that morning
and he presented them to the miners. He invited them to
come to the Abbey that evening to get enough money to
tide them and their families through the critical period of
the strike, and also promised to do everything in his power
to get the strike settled. It was a wonderful example of
choosing the right words at the right time and having the
courage to say them convincingly.

Except for the gentlemen who hunted, luncheon was
served to the guests in the dining room much in the same
fashion as breakfast. We footmen assisted them from our
stations at the sideboard which held roast game in season,
leg of lamb, game pie, roast chicken, and roast ham. There
were always platters of eggs Rochambeau, fish, a garnished
entrée of chicken en gelée, and salad. The dessert was often
rice pudding, which Her Grace enjoyed very much. Only
white wines and claret were served, and the coffee and
liqueurs were served in the drawing room.

After luncheon, most of the guests retired to their rooms.
The more energetic went walking, or cycling, or played
golf.

Then at five o'clock everyone again attended tea. This
was served in the large drawing room and the Duchess
herself presided at the table. It was customary for the
ladies to wear tea gowns and Her Grace was usually attired in a gown of pale blue satin with a Medici collar of
lace, which she seemed to favor, and a corsage of Malmaison
carnations. The Duchess of Sutherland, also a great beauty,
made a lovely picture at another table as she served the
coffee and chocolate. Among the guests were the Archbishop of York (Cosmo Lang), the Duchess of Alba, the

Duchess of Manchester, the German Ambassador, and Grand Duke Alexis, whose tea was prepared in a separate samovar, which he drank with—of all things—lemon!

The younger children, Lady Victoria and little Lord Morven, had tea with their parents nearly every day. When there were guests, they were sometimes allowed to be present. The Marquess of Titchfield, the elder son who was at Eton, was granted this privilege more frequently when he was at home. Lady Victoria played the piano very nicely and, like all proud mothers, the Duchess often asked her to perform. Lord Morven would "recite" in English, French, or German to amuse the company, but the children's visit to the world of their elders was short and sweet. They were brought up in the tradition so characteristic of the Victorian era: "children should be seen and not heard," and then—only by request.

However, the Duke and Duchess did not leave their children entirely to the care of Sister Grace, the head governess, the tutor, and the governess who taught them French and German. They lunched with their parents when there were no guests, but dinner was served in the nursery dining room promptly at 6:30. During the day the Duke and Duchess took them cycling and riding. Lady Victoria accompanied her mother on her frequent visits to the old couples in the "Winnings," and to the miners' wives who were having babies, or who had sick children. Evidently Her Grace believed in these errands of kindness to prepare Lady Victoria for her future responsibilities.

At seven-thirty, the dressing gong sounded, and at 8:15 the guests assembled in the Gothic Hall ready for dinner. No cocktails, apéritifs, nor sherry were served. His Grace felt that they dulled the palate and spoiled the taste of the wine. There was never any protocol about the seating at the table unless it was a state dinner, and then it was rigorously followed.

On the table before each place was a silver holder with a menu of the dinner. The cards always bore the crest of the Duke of Portland and they were constantly being replenished by the printer in London. When the chef, Monsieur David, made up the menus, Mr. Spedding passed on them and had them written out in old-fashioned script. Then they were placed on the table by the groom of the chambers. I have remembered the holders and menu cards with nostalgia because they, more than any other detail, represented the perfect service dispensed at Welbeck.

I am sure that there are few houses today which are still run as Welbeck was then, because such a thing would be impossible unless a whole way of life were recreated. Time has altered many things: most of the great homes have changed hands, and in this restless world of ours, there is neither the wealth nor the patience for such exquisite details.

Among the guests at Welbeck was the Duchess of Manchester. Her arrival was an anticipated event. We all looked forward to seeing her because she was a commanding and unique person, and we were all fond of her footman, Black Jack, as she called him.

She would drive up to Welbeck in her own car driven by her chauffeur, attended by her personal maid and footman. She brought her own mattress, linens, her particular brand of tea, and a special kind of brown bread made of whole-wheat kernels, which she thought kept her healthy.

She was very fussy about everything that had to do with her service, especially about hot plates at dinner. Her own footman waited on her (Black Jack worked smoothly with the four of us but served only the Duchess of Manchester) no matter how many other guests there might be.

Black Jack was tall and prepossessing. He was swarthy and he looked as though he had forgotten to shave. His powdered hair contrasted so markedly with his complexion that he looked like a handsome mulatto. But his disposition was often unpredictable, so there was invariably a crisis with his employer. Black Jack would displease the Duchess and she would discharge him, and then in her next breath she would issue a casual command as though nothing had happened. This turnabout had been going on for years, and I don't think Black Jack himself knew how long he had served the Duchess.

One night at dinner, the Duchess of Manchester was furious because her fish plate was not hot enough. Black Jack came into the serving pantry and he said,

"I'll make it *hot* for her! This is going to be the *hottest* plate there ever was—all right, all right!"

He immersed the silver plate in a pan of boiling water until it was scalding hot, rushed into the dining room, and set it before the Duchess with a serving pad. Her Grace put her fingers on it and let out a shriek because she had burned herself.

"This plate is *too* hot," she screamed, as she wet the tips of her fingers with her tongue. "And you are *dismissed!*"

But nothing disconcerted Jack and he said, loudly enough for all to hear, "I will leave immediately, but I will leave with the satisfaction that Your Grace has really had a *hot* plate at last."

In the course of their stay, Jack was the favorite of the visiting staff and he spent a good deal of his time in the menservants' billiard room. He was popular and everyone liked to drink with him. We arranged a party for him at the Worksop Inn which included some of the housemaids and stillroom maids. I invited Gertrude to be my partner, and Jack took one of the pretty, young stillroom maids. He drank too much and behaved outrageously, but Hales and I managed to get him to bed so that he would be fit for duty in the morning.

Somehow the news of Black Jack's behavior reached the Duchess of Manchester and he was summoned by Her Grace early in the morning. When Jack appeared before her, she said:

"I have heard that you behaved disgracefully last night. Black Jack, is this quite true?"

"I regret to say it is, Your Grace," he replied.

"Why must you drink in such an indelicate manner?" she demanded.

"Your Grace," Jack replied, "if I wasn't drunk some of the time, I don't think I could stand being your footman!"

"You may consider yourself dismissed and you will leave immediately!" the Duchess said icily.

Jack went to his room and prepared to pack his things, his regular course of procedure in these crises. But he went about it now in a more determined manner than usual, and we thought that the straw had finally broken the camel's back.

Imagine my surprise when, twenty minutes later, I answered the Blue Library bell and saw the Duchess of Manchester seated at a desk. She was holding a letter which she tapped on the palm of her hand.

"Gorst," she said blithely, "would you please find Black Jack, my footman, and tell him that I would like him to post an important letter for me in Worksop immediately?"

"Yes, Your Grace, I will deliver your message to your footman as quickly as possible." And I could hardly contain my laughter.

Count Apponyi, who was one of the finest shots on the Continent, was also a frequent guest at Welbeck. Hales had been assigned to him as his footman for the duration of his visit. The Count had made a recent trip to the United States and there he had acquired the idea that his valet should not only keep his wardrobe in shape, but also press his trousers as well.

English servants never pressed gentlemen's clothes in those days. We kept the original crease of the trousers sharp by wet brushing. The coats were also wet-brushed and carefully hung on form-shaped hangers. It was fashionable to have a single trouser crease, even though King Edward VII had encouraged two side creases both for uniforms and civil clothes as a new style.

On this visit the Count ordered Hales to press his clothes and Hales, who knew nothing about pressing, told him politely it was not customary. The Count accepted this explanation but he shook his head in exasperation.

"In these matters," he said, "it appears that American valets are much less old-fashioned than you! Why don't you learn to use an iron?"

The day Count Apponyi was leaving, he ordered Hales to

go to the telegrapher's office to send a telegram to London. The Count gave him a shilling, and after the telegram had been sent, Hales returned with the change. Count Apponyi was in the Gothic Hall ready to leave with the other guests.

Hales put the sixpence on a silver salver and approached Count Apponyi.

"Your change from the telegram, Count Apponyi," Hales said bowing low.

"Oh, that is for you," the Count replied.

Hales realized that the Count intended the coin as his tip for looking after him, and like Black Jack, Hales had spunk. He was impervious to embarrassment.

"I couldn't possibly accept this," Hales said drawing himself up to his full six feet, three. "I suggest, Count Apponyi, that *you* keep the sixpence. You might want to send another telegram."

The Count flushed and said nothing. Then he dug down in his pocket and presented Hales with a sovereign.

All of the guests at Welbeck were most generous with those who served them and this incident was the exception to the rule. I could imagine someone offering a sixpence to Askew, or Osborn, or me—but not to *Hales!*

Among the other distinguished visitors who came to Welbeck was Mr. Joseph Chamberlain. Every day Mr. Chamberlain went for a walk with an orchid in his buttonhole and a monocle in his eye. At the end of the week that he spent as the guest of the Duke and Duchess of Portland, he was scheduled to give a speech in the Riding School.

For six days, the carpenters worked to install stands so that the huge ring would be converted into an auditorium in time for the event. Thousands of people came to hear him and a buffet luncheon was served to a great number of guests who stayed to meet Mr. Chamberlain after he had delivered his address and received an ovation. This was the largest luncheon party ever given during my service at Welbeck.

But the excitement generated by Mr. Chamberlain's presence was mild compared to the furor created when a telephone message arrived from Chatsworth House announcing that Their Majesties, King Edward VII and Queen Alexandra, would arrive at Welbeck the next day for luncheon. This was, of course, in the nature of a Royal command. When Mr. Spedding received his orders, we went into action like the Royal Fusiliers going into battle.

The only other guests at this time were the Duke and Duchess of Sutherland, so that the luncheon was small and unusually informal. After the meal had been served, the ladies withdrew with the Queen and her lady in waiting. Askew and I waited upon the gentlemen. I was serving the Duke of Portland a liqueur when I heard His Majesty say to him:

"This is indeed one of the most delightful and comfortable houses I have ever been in."

Even a king could not fail to recognize the grandeur of Welbeck Abbey.

However there were days, even weeks, when things moved along at a more leisurely pace, when the Duke and Duchess were absorbed with their own personal responsibilities. The Duchess held a fortnightly sewing class at the Abbey for the miners' wives, and with an instructress, showed them how to make baby clothes, layettes, dresses, and embroidery work. At five o'clock, tea was served for everyone in the large dining room, and Her Grace sat at the head of the table serving the tea herself from the silver urn. Askew and I passed the sandwiches and cakes to which the ladies helped themselves liberally.

A little old lady sitting next to the Duchess asked if she might have another cup of tea. Her Grace took the cup and poured the dregs into the silver slop bowl on the tray. The miner's wife looked amazed while she watched this process and she said,

"Oh—is that what you do with the slops?"

"Why, what do *you* do with them?" the Duchess asked politely.

"Oh, I just chuck them in the fire, M'um," she said.

"It is really much easier to put them in a bowl, do you agree with me?" Her Grace said kindly.

"I must get me a crockery one for when we have tea, and learn to use it," the lady answered.

Her Grace smiled kindly, and I could see how touched and amused she was by her teatime pupil's response. She enjoyed helping, in many ways, the women who came for the sewing session. Not only did she help them with their clothes but she also offered suggestions about their houses and gardens, and even about small matters of taste and manners.

We servants took a dimmer view of the sewing class than the Duchess. All of us thought that the miners' wives were funny and we derived a good deal of amusement from these gatherings. When they came to the Abbey as the guests of the Duchess, some of them treated the servants with the utmost disdain and snubbed us as though they were Duchesses themselves. Others were shy and uncomfortable in such august surroundings, and were humble almost to the point of embarrassment.

Before the ladies left, they formed a line to use the lavatory, and none of them missed the opportunity to see the lavish bathrooms, try the hot and cold running water, and use the luxurious soap and the embroidered towels.

I suppose we servants were all very unkind, but many of us found we suddenly had tasks to do in the vicinity in order to hear the comments and conversation. But even though we laughed at the miners' ladies, we knew how seriously Her Grace took these afternoons, and any disrespect that we might have overtly shown them would have brought a sharp rebuke from the Duchess.

The generosity of the Duke and Duchess seemed boundless. They even allowed a band of Gypsies to make a camp on the estate not far from Worksop. Many of the servants, mostly the maids, went to have their fortunes told. The Gypsy women would predict a brilliant future if you gave them a large enough coin. Jim and I heard that they were giving a play, and on our evening off we bicycled to the Gypsy encampment.

The Gypsy caravan had a beautiful collection of wagons. Some of them were carved with designs of griffons, boar's heads, and bunches of grapes. The scrolled doors and all of the shutters were made by hand. The side of one of the wagons opened up and cleverly formed a stage. It was here that the King of the Gypsies and some of the women of the caravan gave their playlet.

The King was the star of the show. He was a handsome young man with black curly hair that set off his sunburned skin. He wore gold hoop earrings in his pierced ears, a pair of high crushed suede boots, and a costume that might have belonged to a matador. The effect was startling. He was a brilliant actor, and the play, a Romany version of the "Carmen" story, was magically effective against the sky and the stars as a backdrop for the miniature wagon stage and the colorful, outlandish costumes.

After the play, Jim and I lingered to compliment the attractive Gypsy King on his performance. He seemed so pleased that we had bothered to congratulate him that he invited us to stay for supper. We went into his own wagon, which had a gilded door and wonderfully handsome carriage lamps which he told us he had made himself. I was inclined to believe him because the Gypsies were famous not only for their music but for their excellence in metal work.

The wagon was a charming little place done with a great deal of taste, even to a small fireplace where a fire was burning. The Gypsy King offered us whiskey before dinner, and the table was nicely set for three. He had a dresser and a valet who also served his meals.

One dish of the meal was really outstanding. It appeared to be a most tastefully prepared chicken, and we asked him how it was cooked. He laughed uproariously and said:

"I am sorry to disappoint you, my dear friends, but you have just eaten a hedgehog!"

We were even more intrigued when he told us that the animal was rolled in clay immediately after it was killed. Then it was placed in the fire and baked until the ball of clay slowly started to open. At this point, all of the skin and spines peeled away with the clay and nothing remained but the perfectly roasted white meat.

We invited the King to return our visit and urged him to come to Welbeck for an evening. He politely declined our invitation, saying that he was much too busy keeping his people out of trouble—that a Gypsy King could not travel unmolested about the countryside because most of the villagers would misunderstand his presence.

"We are not very well regarded by the miners and peasants," he continued. "They suspect us of all kinds of evil intentions, like stealing, and kidnapping their children. It is safer for me to stay here. You are welcome to visit my caravan at any time. It would be an honor."

Jim and I never saw the young Gypsy King again. I should have had my fortune told the night we saw the play; perhaps some clairvoyant Gypsy woman could have prophesied my disillusionment, and like some dark-eyed sibyl, predicted that a blue-eyed temptress would soon deceive me.

There were a great number of guests at Welbeck, so there were also a large number of visiting servants, among them a good-looking young German chauffeur who drove the German Ambassador. He was tall, blond, and handsome and he created quite a stir among the housemaids. I had not realized to what degree he had impressed the young ladies on the staff until the morning that I went, as usual, to the stillroom to get the rolls and bread for luncheon. As I entered the stillroom, I found my darling Gertrude sitting on the young German chauffeur's lap! I couldn't believe my eyes, but I managed to say:

"I hope I'm not intruding."

They both laughed loudly, and Gertrude said airily,

"No indeed, Fred, you're not intruding. Not in the least!"

I was deeply shocked by her brazen answer and I retreated to nurse my badly hurt feelings in the footmen's pantry, where Askew was waiting for the bread to put it on the table. As I came in he looked up.

"What's the matter, Fred? You're white as a ghost!"

I told him what I had seen and Jim interrupted my tirade with some ideas of his own.

"If you want to know, Fred, what I think—this is the best thing that could have happened to you. We have all known for a long time what a coy minx your beloved Gertrude is. And now you've seen it for yourself! She is vain and selfish, and perhaps this will teach you not to be taken in by a pretty face."

For several weeks I nursed what I thought was a "broken heart," but when one is young that state of mind is temporary. Whenever it was my duty to go to the stillroom to collect the bread, I was upset by her presence, but even that began to wear off. It wasn't long before I recovered from "Wing'd Cupid's darts." Jim was a great help to me because he had much more worldly wisdom. He knew all about the intrigues and love affairs which constantly went on among the staff and he understood how transitory and fleeting most of these flirtations were.

As Christmas approached, we were so busy that I had no time for dalliance or regret. There were between twenty and thirty guests over Christmas and New Year's, and the continuous house party required a great deal of service.

The Abbey was magnificently decorated with holly foliage and pine garlands, and the great halls were banked

with flowering Christmas plants which had been brought
in from the hothouses. Christmas Eve was a gala affair for
the family and their close friends, and when they had exchanged their own gifts, the Duke and Duchess presented
each of the Royal footmen with an envelope which was
sealed in wax with the Portland crest. When I opened
mine I discovered that I was richer by a five-pound note.

The great event, a ball for the staff, always took place
on Twelfth-night, the eve of the 6th of January, commemorating the feast of Epiphany, the conclusion of the
Christmas observances in ancient times.

It was held in the underground ballroom and the three
great reception rooms. The rooms were beautifully decorated, just as though the Duke and Duchess were giving a
ball for themselves. The flowering plants were brought
down and there were arbors of potted palms and ferns.
The skylights in the lawn had been slightly opened and
the ventilation was as perfect as if the entire area had been
air-conditioned.

All of the staff, the tenants on the estate and their
families, and the tradesmen in Worksop and their wives
had been invited. There were about 1,200 guests for the
ball and they were easily accommodated in the palatial
rooms. An orchestra from London had been engaged and a
swarm of 50 waiters arrived to take over the service, because none of us was required to perform any duties that
evening—this was the social event of *our* season!

One reception room had been set up as a cloak room for
the ball, and the other huge rooms were arranged with
tables for the midnight supper. There were pine festoons

on the great chandeliers and hundreds of small gilt chairs with red velvet seats lined the ballroom walls.

When the Duke and Duchess arrived, Osborne, Hales, Askew, and I followed in their wake as proud as peacocks to attend them for their entrance. We wore our epaulet liveries because we were, in a sense, still on duty, but it had been previously arranged that as soon as the Duke and Duchess left, we would be permitted to go to our rooms and put on our own full dress clothes.

Everyone was in evening dress and it was quite a revelation to see all of the members of the staff in ball dress. Even the prim head housemaid looked quite chic in a velvet gown, and the head housekeeper, who wore a low-cut blue satin gown, was almost unrecognizable without her stiff, black silk dress and her belt of jingling keys.

Many members of the staff looked so well in their ball clothes that it sparked off the party; and, as I looked around, I found that we had acquired a new kind of individuality and gaiety for the evening, and stranger still, that we were seeing each other from a new aspect—as people, not as servants.

The Duchess opened the ball by dancing with Mr. Spedding, and as hundreds of couples followed them on to the ballroom floor, the grand event was in full swing. Naturally the Duchess was the most majestic figure in the ballroom. She had on a magnificent ecru satin gown, embroidered with white passementerie and pearls almost as large as those in the fabulous "dog collar" about her neck. She wore a spectacular ruby and diamond crescent on her hair and matching pendant ruby earrings. She was the epitome of feminine elegance.

During supper, the Duke and Duchess made a pretence of having a bite but they left the ball room soon after midnight.

Everything was served from a buffet and the entire silver service was used. Champagne was consumed in unlimited quantities, and the dancing and merrymaking continued until the small hours. With the coming of dawn all of the Cinderellas were reminded that this was another day of work, and that the most exciting party of the year was rapidly drawing to a close.

In the morning, the Duke and Duchess left for a week to visit friends, partly, I am sure, for their own enjoyment, but certainly to permit the staff to recover from the ball and allow all the excitement to simmer down into the methodical, established routine.

By the time they returned, the effects of the ball had worn off and everyone was once more in the line of duty. The finest Servants' Ball in England was over for another year.

14

Windsor Castle

THE Duke and Duchess of Portland remained at Welbeck Abbey from October until June. The weather was usually quite mild, with not too much snow but a good bit of rain and fog. Still, I looked foward to the coming of spring because I knew that the gardens, great oaks and surrounding woods would be a joy to behold.

When April finally came, Jim and I took advantage of every moment on our days off. We dressed ourselves in very sporting attire: knickerbockers, low shoes, long knee socks, and tweed jackets and caps, and took off on our bikes to tour the countryside. In May we visited the villages near Worksop, which were almost entirely rows of miners' cottages. They were built of stone, lining the narrow streets so closely that the rambler roses twining over them seemed one continuous mass of color.

One afternoon, we stopped to see the remains of Hardwick Hall about twenty miles away. This fine old house was in ruins, and the saying was: "Hardwick Hall—more glass than wall." It had been the home of "Building Bess of Hardwick," who, as Lady Cavendish, had first owned Welbeck Abbey and rebuilt part of it. We also went to see Worksop Manor, another of Building Bess' architectural accomplishments while she was the wife of the Earl of Shrewsbury. It was here that Mary Queen of Scots had been imprisoned for many miserable months in a room just off the main staircase. The old caretaker mechanically droned out this information as part of his guided tour.

When we told him that we were Royal footmen at Welbeck, he invited us to take a cup of tea with him. The Duke and Duchess were held in such high esteem by the people in the countryside that it was an "open sesame" just to say you served them.

By the beginning of June, we were all preoccupied with preparations for returning to London for the season. In the midst of our activities, Mr. Spedding gave the four Royal footmen orders to report to Windsor Castle for duty at the wedding of Princess Margaret of Connaught to Crown Prince Gustave Adolphus of Sweden.

This was to be the first time that I would serve at Windsor Castle. Although I tried not to show it, I was trembling like a schoolboy when Osborn, Hales, Askew, and I took the train to Windsor together. As we drove into the Home Park, I saw the tower of the castle in the distance. This was what I had been waiting and working for—the Royal service. As we continued through the park where the gently sloping land was still covered by stands of the old Royal Forest, and neared the lawns and terraces which rose toward the castle itself, I felt that I was about to realize the dream of a lifetime.

We went to see St. George's Chapel where the wedding

was to take place. It was the historic chapel of the Knights of the Garter, and in its vaults King Henry VIII and Jane Seymour, George III, and many other sovereigns were entombed. Above the dark oak stalls, in colorful array, hung shiny helmets, banners, and swords of the Knights of the Garter—eloquent epitaphs to England's past.

At ten-thirty the next morning, the procession of carriages began to form outside Windsor Castle to proceed straight to St. George's Chapel for the wedding.

Princess Margaret was the first to arrive in her carriage with her father, H.R.H. Prince Arthur, Duke of Connaught, the brother of His Majesty, King Edward VII. She walked up the steps of the chapel on her father's arm, under an arch formed by the javelins of the Beefeaters who stood on the steps as a guard of honor. Then Crown Prince Gustave Adolphus' carriage drove up bearing the Crown Prince and His Majesty, King Edward VII, who served as honorary best man.

Askew and I rode on the back of the carriage for the Duke and Duchess of Portland, and as soon as all the carriages had left the guests at the steps, we were allowed to watch the ceremony from the rear of the chapel.

The bride and groom, Crown Prince Gustave and Princess Margaret, emerged from the chapel wreathed in smiles—just like any other happy, young couple. For us this was a signal to take our places at the backs of the carriages to return to Windsor Castle for the wedding breakfast.

The ceremony took place a little after eleven and when we reached the castle, we were told that there would not be time to change our liveries—we should wait upon the guests in our Ascot uniforms. This was the only time that I waited on table at a full-state function in an Ascot livery.

We were going about the tables in St. George's Hall and the Waterloo Chambers in riding boots, buckskin breeches, and scarlet coats. Despite the novelty of the situation, we all felt that our costumes were more appropriate for a hunt breakfast than a Royal wedding. The occasion demanded a more formal costume, but in the end we must have added color to the already brilliant scene.

The Princess cut the cake, a magnificent tower of twelve tiers, iced in white ornamental roses, with the Crown Prince's sword—just like brides the world over—except that most of them have to be content to cut their wedding cakes with a sharp, silver knife. The first piece of cake was served to Her Majesty, Queen Alexandra, who looked radiantly beautiful that day, almost overshadowing the bride. The second went to His Majesty, King Edward VII, and then the young couple was served.

During the breakfast, they disappeared and where they went, no one knew. Great care had been taken to insure the privacy of their leave-taking. When their departure was eventually noticed, everyone rose to toast their health and happiness.

After the breakfast, the Sergeant Footman brought down twelve quarts of champagne to the footmen's room. We drank a toast, first to Their Majesties, and then to the young couple. No group of loyal British subjects could have wished them better luck than we did.

The second time that I was ordered to Windsor Castle, we were commanded to the carriages to meet the Royal train, which was arriving at Windsor Station with King Carlos and Queen Amelia of Portugal.

The first evening of their visit at Windsor with King Edward VII and Queen Alexandra, there was a small dinner for about thirty people and the evening ended fairly early. But the next day the entertainment began in earnest.

King Carlos, attended by the gentlemen in his suite, and various guests of King Edward's went shooting in the forests. King Carlos was a superb shot. We were told that he carried a small revolver and that he never feared an assassin because he was such an accurate marksman. It is ironical that some years later he, together with his son, the Prince Royal, died from an assassin's bullet.

King Edward VII was not particularly interested in shooting. It was not too difficult to understand why. Such activity hardly went with his figure—he was definitely on the portly side. He was always so beautifully and elegantly turned out that it was hard to imagine him really enjoying a sporting costume.

That evening a large banquet was given. One hundred and fifty guests were served in St. George's Hall with all the Crown gold on display. There were many fascinating pieces of ornamental gold, cups and vases commemorating important events, and fabulous gifts from foreign rulers.

One of the outstanding objects was a golden peacock with its fantail spread, each feather outlined with precious stones. It stood resplendent in the light, and the beauty of the workmanship and the size of the gems made one gasp in wonder. Another piece, a lion's head in solid gold, was captured in India by an English officer and presented to Queen Victoria.

All of the food for the banquet was brought in heated trucks from the kitchen to the dining rooms by the porters. The method of heating them was less efficient than the trolley at Welbeck. At Windsor Castle "iron bricks" were placed in the enormous open fireplace in the kitchen. When they were red hot they were lifted on heavy revolving hooks and placed in the bottom compartment of the food wagons. The bricks kept the food reasonably hot while the wagons were wheeled by hand to the pantries, but they were not completely reliable.

Up to this time, no one had devised a successful method of transporting food in the great houses and castles in England—the distances were too great, and from the moment the food left the stove until it reached the table too many people were involved in the process. At Windsor, we constantly urged the porters to hurry along with the wagons because speed was of the utmost importance.

After the banquet in St. George's Hall was over, the guests adjourned to the Waterloo Chambers where a command performance of "A Man's Shadow" was given by Sir Herbert Beerbohm Tree and his entire company, brought from London just for this evening's performance at Windsor Castle.

The second day was almost a duplicate of the first, but with minor changes in the festivities. There was a picnic in the Royal Forest, and the play in the evening was "Monsieur Beaucaire" with Louis Waller, one of the greatest actors of his time.

According to custom, King Carlos and Queen Amelia prepared to leave early the next morning for a parade and a luncheon to be given in their honor by the Lord Mayor of London.

We left Windsor Castle for the station in the semi-state carriages. There were sixteen footmen and eight coachmen on the carriages. I was on the Duc d'Acosta's carriage, gentleman in waiting to King Carlos.

Going down the hill from Windsor to the station, we had to place our coats over the bar of the carriage platforms in such a way that they would be uniformly draped. As I walked to the train with Askew, he said:

"Fred, you have forgotten your topcoat!"

I dashed back and ran after the carriages as fast as I could. They had already turned about to go back to Windsor, and I finally attracted the attention of the last coachman who heard my frantic cries and stopped the carriages. I retrieved my coat and just made the Royal train as it was beginning to move out of the station.

Askew held the door open and with his help, after a final running leap which landed me on my stomach, I just managed to tumble aboard. If I had lost my coat, there would have been the devil to pay, not to mention the maze of red tape that I would have gone through in the Sergeant Footman's office at Buckingham Palace.

I was not the only footman who got into difficulty on the journey to London. Ramsdale, now a senior footman at the Palace and the most recent "graduate" from the four Royal footmen, shared our compartment. He was a quiet, contained chap who went about his business with the greatest assurance and a minimum of fuss. Ramsdale was sitting reading a book as usual. Suddenly he let out a shout and his face grew ashen.

"Hales! Osborn! One of you chaps—please help me!" he cried. "I think I have a cramp in my leg. I have to get my boot off!"

Four of us scrambled out of our seats and ran to his assistance. Hales tried to pull the high black boot off. I knew that would only add to the pain, so I reached into my hand valise and brought out my pocket knife.

"Good boy!" Hales said. "Hand it to me and we'll soon have that boot off."

He took the sharp edge and slit Ramsdale's boot neatly down the back seam. As soon as the boot flared open, Ramsdale was able to bend his leg. After a few moments, the cramp subsided. And so did the confusion.

Then we realized there wasn't a spare pair of boots among us and that Ramsdale would have to wear the ludicrous object standing on the floor.

"How can I wear that thing!" he said. "It was easy to cut it open, but how will I manage to hold it together?"

"Well, you'll have to wear it as it is," Hales said. "You'll just have to be 'Old Slit Boot' for the parade!"

We all ragged poor Ramsdale, but he took it in good grace. He was lucky as well as good tempered, because I found an old Gladstone tie in my valise when I put my knife away. So I anchored it around the boot and saved the day.

When we arrived in London at Paddington Station, we were met by the same number of carriages, and we took our places as they had been assigned at Windsor. Then the parade began with a drive through some of the boroughs of London. According to custom, King Edward VII and Queen Alexandra did not participate in the parade. When we arrived at the Guild Hall, King Carlos was officially greeted by the Lord Mayor of London and presented with a gold key to the city.

The guests assembled in the Guild Hall for luncheon, and in an anteroom of the main dining room a table was set up for the footmen and coachmen. We were served the same dishes as the Royal visitors, beginning with turtle soup and ending with the choicest strawberries and champagne.

As soon as we had finished, we took our places outside on the steps of Guild Hall to await King Carlos and Queen Amelia and their attendants. In our own terminology, we were waiting for the "Royals."

Askew and I stood at the foot of the steps awaiting the signal which we would relay to the coachmen to bring up the carriages. Suddenly a jaunty young fellow, wearing a square bowler hat and carrying a briefcase, came up to me and said:

"When are they coming out?"

"I don't know yet, sir. We haven't been informed," I answered.

"That's peculiar—" he said, pushing his lower lip upward and thrusting his chin forward. "Isn't it your business to know when they are expected?"

I was annoyed by this remark because it was impossible for me to know exactly when the luncheon would be over. Turning to a man who was standing next to me I said,

"Who the devil is he—and who does he *think* he is?"

"He is a very bright young man," my informant answered, "and right now he's a Liberal rebel who's giving the Conservatives a run for their money. His name is Winston Churchill."

When the Royal visitors emerged from the Guild Hall, Jim and I gave the signal and the carriages drove up in order. Then the procession drove back to Paddington Station, where we again accompanied King Carlos and Queen Amelia back to Windsor Castle on the Royal train.

The shooting parties, dinners, banquets, and entertainments continued for a week at Windsor, and then we were commanded back to Welbeck because the Duke and Duchess of Portland had invited King Carlos and Queen Amelia to visit them the following week.

The Royal guests occupied the State Apartment at Welbeck. They spent many hours inspecting the Abbey and they seemed to be enthusiastic about everything they saw.

One evening while I was on hall duty, the Duke of Portland and King Carlos entered the Gothic Hall. I sat in my accustomed place in a chair behind the screen. When I heard His Grace's familiar "hello," I came out to see what he wished.

"Gorst, I have opened the wine tantalus. Will you pour the brandy?" the Duke requested. "Pull out the cigar shelves so that His Majesty may help himself."

I opened the beautiful cabinet by lifting the lid. As it moved upward, two shelves on brass levers rose up out of the center. Four crystal decanters, and a variety of glasses and goblets fitted into the grooves, meticulously covered with green felt. Below the shelves, movable trays, holding Havana cigars and specially blended Turkish cigarettes, came up at the touch of a finger.

King Carlos stood beside me examining the appurtenances and fittings, fascinated by the ingenious construction.

"It is a truly remarkable box," he said to His Grace. "Many useful objects are well adapted to a small space, and it is beautifully made. Why do you call it a 'tantalus'?"

"I think the word comes from Tantalus, who was a cruel king in Roman mythology," the Duke said. "To punish his crimes, the gods immersed him in water up to his chin, with a branch of luscious fruit hanging down over his head. When he wanted to eat, the fruit eluded him; when he wanted to drink, the water receded. Thus, for the rest of eternity, he endured this singular torture."

"I see," King Carlos replied. "But this handsome cabinet surely provides no such punishment."

"You would be astonished how *tantalizing* it can be," His Grace said laughingly. "When I am displeased with the footman on duty, I close the lid with the combination locked. But when I am feeling amiable, I leave it open—which is most of the time—so that the footman can have a whiskey before he goes to bed."

Both His Grace and King Carlos smiled at me as I went back to my chair behind the screen.

When the fortnight of festivities had passed, I was so exhausted from the work and the excitement that I wondered how King Carlos and Queen Amelia, the Duke and Duchess of Portland, and all the guests who partook of these endless entertainments felt when it was over! So much food, so much drink, and so much conversation! Surely they must have been tired too! I often wondered if they were bored or satiated by the pursuit of so much pleasure. But it was my job to serve and I did so—tired or no.

However, I had one complaint which most of the footmen shared—"Windsor feet." The Royal corridors were carpeted but the servants' corridors were bare stone, and there seemed to be miles of them. The distances were enormous, from the servants' quarters to the footmen's room, from the kitchens to the dining rooms—I don't know how many miles a day we walked. No wonder we all took foot baths at night!

However our services did not go unrewarded. The Comptroller of the Household distributed five pounds from King Carlos to each footman who had served him or a member of his entourage. Later it came to our ears that King Carlos had intended to have commemorative medals struck for us, bearing a portrait of himself and Queen Amelia. He discussed the plan with the Comptroller, who vetoed the idea, stating flatly that the footmen would prefer a gift in money. This report blew up a tempest in the footmen's pantry, and while the heated discussion was in progress, a somewhat similar incident was recalled.

During Queen Victoria's reign, an Indian prince had been Her Majesty's guest at Buckingham Palace. Shortly before he left, he requested the Comptroller to buy gold cuff links for the footmen who had served him. The Comptroller refused, saying that it was unnecessary to reward the servants, who were amply paid for their services. The incident created a furor, eventually coming to the attention of Queen Victoria herself.

She summoned the Comptroller and asked why the prince's request had not been carried out. It was said that Her Majesty remarked tartly,

"And, sir, did you see fit to refuse the jeweled box His

Highness gave you? I would like to have the gold cuff links given to all the footmen who earned them."

Since that time, there has been no question about the propriety of foreign visitors presenting gifts to members of the Palace staff, and the practice was continued by King Edward VII.

Although I had no commemorative medal to add to the collection, I did send a few unofficial souvenirs of King Carlos' visit to my sister, Lily. She always enjoyed the mementos of my Royal service. This time I sent her the programs of the performances of Sir Herbert Beerbohm Tree and Louis Waller. They were made of silk and resembled small Chinese scrolls. I also enclosed the program of the string orchestra concerts given during dinner, and the menu of the great banquet held on the second evening of King Carlos' visit. I continued to send Lily souvenirs like this as long as I was in the Royal service.

One of the most colorful events in England was the Royal Ascot. Although there were other great tracks in England, like Epsom Downs where the Derby was run, and Aintree, the scene of the Grand National Steeplechase, Ascot was the only event which Their Majesties officially attended. Consequently, it was the most gala of all such occasions.

That year the Duke and Duchess of Portland were invited to be the guests of King Edward and Queen Alexandra at Windsor Castle to attend Ascot Week. So, we Royal footmen had been ordered to Windsor Castle for duty.

Hales was the busiest. He went back and forth between

London and Windsor almost every day. He left in the evening and returned in the early afternoon of the next day carrying a pyramid of boxes, beautifully wrapped with fancy paper and satin ribbons. These contained an array of dresses and hats for Her Grace's wardrobe. During the week I observed that she never wore the same costume twice.

Thursday of Ascot Week was Gold Cup Day, and it was the custom for all of the ladies to reserve their most beautiful gowns for this final climax to the week's glittering display of elegance. The weather was unpredictable, so several costumes had to be ready for any changes in temperature.

On the first day of the meet, the carriages left Windsor Castle with two postillion riders who guided the near horse, controlling the other one with auxiliary reins. On arriving at the track, the carriages all drove to the Royal box which was in the Royal Pavilion. After the guests had alighted, the carriages were taken to the Royal stables at the back of the track. All of the footmen went into the serving rooms in the pavilion to prepare for the luncheon and afternoon reception which Their Majesties gave each day.

One afternoon while I was in the serving pantry straightening up after the luncheon, an old bookie, named Bruce, stopped by to see us. In England, in those days, there were several kinds of bookies in the profession. There were "high-class bookies," there were the "grandstand bookies" who were really put on their honor to pay their debts, and there were the "field bookies." The "field" was on the opposite side of the grandstand, and there anyone could come in free. Many people took advantage of this opportunity and they brought their own picnics and had a fine jamboree.

But they took pot luck if they were adventuresome enough to bet with the "field bookies!" These gentlemen were more distinguished for their numbers than their honor. Once in a while one of them would renege on a bet and a hullabaloo would go up on the field, and shouts of "Welcher! Welcher!" would carry across the track. The crowd would mob them and the track police would have to intervene to save these rum blokes' skins!

But Bruce was a cut above these ordinary chaps. Although he may have started as a field bookie, by the time I met him he was known as quite an "operator."

" 'ello there, Gorst, old boy," he greeted me. " 'ow goes it? Any chance of a little snifter?"

I handed him the remnants of a bottle of champagne and said, "Brucie, this should make you feel fit."

"This is exactly what I need. I 'ad a bad night last night. And now, just for your kindness, I'm going to give you and Haskew a good tip on the race! Bet everything you've got on the Duke's 'Greendale Oak.' "

Askew and I began to laugh because we recognized the name of the horse.

"The Duke of *who?*" I said.

"Why, the Duke of Portland, of course! You know who owns 'Greendale Oak.' You're just pulling my leg." And Bruce couldn't figure out if we were laughing with him or at him.

"I'm so sure you'll win that I'll let you in on a secret. I've sent all my money to 'olland (he was dropping "H's" faster than tips) to cover my bet on the Duke's 'orse. I'm getting better hodds in 'olland than they're giving 'ere. I'll give you a piece of my bet."

I don't know what perverse impulse possessed us, perhaps a curious kind of loyalty, but Jim and I gave Bruce ten pounds. However, this was one time when His Grace's entry did not win the race, and late that afternoon we returned to Windsor Castle with empty purses. The occasion, for all its glamor, contained a moral. If you bet on horses, even the Duke of Portland's, you must be prepared to lose.

CHAPTER

15

The King's Dinner

WHEN it came time to leave Welbeck to return to London for the season, the strawberries were ripe in the garden beds. A staff of stillroom maids who stayed during the summer and early autumn did the preserving. The gardeners brought in the fruits as they ripened, and the strawberries were made into the most delicious jam. What their recipe was—I don't know—but the berries, somehow, were always kept whole.

Many years later I searched for a comparable jam and I found only one that was anything like it: Mission Garden. There are many dishes, relishes, and preserves that are famous, but I think the English have always excelled in making jams and jellies.

My duties took me back to 3 Grosvenor Square. The London season had already begun. The Duke of Portland attended His Majesty's Levées, and the Duke and Duchess were present for all of the state occasions at Buckingham Palace: the Drawing Rooms or Presentations, the Garden Party, the Court Balls, and all of the events for King Alphonso's visit. The Duke and Duchess entertained at tea or dinner almost every day. But the great event at 3 Grosvenor Square was the dinner which the Duke gave for His Majesty, King Edward VII.

The excitement began when the entire collection of gold plate, which was to be used for the dinner, came from Welbeck crated and laced with steel bands. It was guarded on the train by Mr. Owens, the underbutler, and two armed detectives. Two special vans transported it from the station, and the menservants in the house formed a cordon as it was carried into the pantries.

For the King's dinner (gentlemen only) it was customary to set up a large oval table because His Majesty preferred it that way. He liked to sit exactly in the center of one side of the oval and face his host, the Duke of Portland, directly opposite him. The rest of the gentlemen sat anywhere they wished without special designation as to rank. His Majesty realized that humor and wit rarely flourished in an atmosphere of strict protocol.

When the Duke had passed on the menu which Mr. Spedding and Monsieur David, the chef, had devised, the menu cards for the King's dinner went to press. They were somewhat larger than those used for the ordinary dinners of the household. Printed in gilt on a red, white, and blue edged card, they featured the Portland crest emblazoned at the top.

This was the menu. The italics are the instructions to the footmen, my comments are bracketed.

Clear Turtle Soup .... *Serve with a dry Sherry.*

Poached Turbot ...... *Serve with oyster sauce and Rhine wine.*

Chicken en Truffles ... *Begin to serve champagne.*
Sous Cloche

Beef with Yorkshire
   Pudding .... *Begin to serve claret.*
Vegetables

Egyptian Quail with
Red Currant Jelly .... *Continue to serve claret.*

Salade au Nature ..... *Serve on a crescent, glass plate fitted exactly next to the dinner plate. Continue with claret.*

Strawberry Trifle .... *Serve champagne.*

Savory .... *Begin to serve one vintage*
(Scotch woodcock— *port.* (The purpose of this
grated eggs on toast dish was to "take away" the
with cheese and an- cloying taste of the dessert,
chovy paste) or sweet.)

Ice and Petits Fours ... (Elaborate forms of ices in various flavors)
   Serve small gateaux and champagne.

Fruit .... *Serve tall compote dishes with all kinds of fresh fruit. Serve grapes. Serve three kinds of vintage port.*
   (varying as to dryness).

Coffee .... *Coffee at table.*
   Serve brandy, cigars, and cigarettes.

The head gardener from Welbeck was in charge of the floral decorations. The house was magnificently decorated and adorned with flowers and plants that had been brought to London from the greenhouses at Welbeck. In order to allow His Majesty to have an unbroken view, a kind of double track of low trays filled with purple and white orchids and ferns crossed the entire length of the table. The gold candelabras were so placed that they did not interrupt his vision from one end of the table to the other.

On this occasion, Mr. Spedding took over the table setting as well as the menu. The underbutler, the groom of the chambers, Osborn, Hales, Askew and I assisted him.

There were never service plates used in the sense that we have them today. When the guests came to the table, the gold flat service was laid at each place, including a soup spoon, two forks, and two pistol knives (so called because of the shape of the handles). A large napkin occupied the center of each place, elegantly folded in a style called the "Bishop's mitre."

Ordinarily we used the "lazy footman" style, but in either instance, the bread was put into the shell-like flap of the napkin.

For a dinner with so many courses, it was impossible to have the table set with all of the utensils, so after the initial forks and knives had been used, we had to lay more of them as they were needed. After the savory, we cleared the table for the ice and fruit.

The spectacular feature of the fruit course was a magnificent bunch of grapes from the Welbeck vinery, beautifully displayed with leaves and flowers on an enormous gold platter. The grapes were a prize bunch and weighed almost eighteen pounds.

Fifty guests were expected for the dinner and there was a staff of twenty-five footmen to wait upon them. We four Royal footmen and the additional Palace footmen, who were on duty for the evening, wore epaulet livery, even on this occasion, because state and full-state uniforms were never worn outside of Buckingham Palace. The order of service had been carefully worked out both from the point of view of efficiency and psychology. Each footman was allowed to wait on His Majesty at least once during the dinner. I was designated to hand him the game.

After His Majesty and his equerry arrived, dinner was announced almost immediately, since no apéritifs were served. Once His Majesty and the Duke of Portland had taken their places, the other guests seated themselves at random. Within several minutes the covered soup tureens had been placed on the table—and the dinner began.

Whenever I had a free moment I studied His Majesty. He was indeed a handsome man with his pointed beard and slightly protruding but perceptive eyes. I noticed that his hair was graying, that he was markedly aging, and that he was even more portly than when I had first seen him at Welbeck.

He seemed in no mood for serious conversation, although he did make an interesting prophecy. The conversation was centered on an amazing exploit in the United States. Two daring men had successfully driven across the continent in an automobile—from San Francisco to New York. His Majesty said he was firmly convinced that, in the years to come, the automobile would influence the national economy as much as the industrial revolution. Although the gentlemen nodded in polite agreement, I felt that some of them did not share His Majesty's opinion.

When I served him the game, he handled the utensils deftly and executed a perfect passage of the quail from the platter to his plate. I was pleased with his gracious smile which seemed to acknowledge my service. He helped himself liberally to everything, particularly enjoying the excellent wines, which he savored and sniffed before drinking. When the port wine was served His Majesty tasted the three different vintages before making his choice.

When it came time for the fruit to be served, Mr. Spedding took the gold platter bearing the prize bunch of grapes from the table to a special serving stand set up in the pantry alcove. Then he returned to the table to get the gold grape scissors in order to cut the huge bunch into small clusters so that they could be served individually.

When he went back to the alcove, the grapes were gone. He let out a shout, "Shut the pantry doors—someone has stolen the grapes!"

The Duke of Portland heard the commotion and beckoned to me.

"Gorst," he said in a whisper, "please go and ask Mr. Spedding what this is all about."

I delivered the message, and Mr. Spedding, angry and agitated, hurried back into the dining room.

"Your Grace, the grapes have disappeared," he said to the Duke. "I simply can't account for it!"

"It does seem odd," His Grace replied. "But have the other fruits served and let's not have any further disturbance."

After the coffee was served, the gentlemen remained at the table for about an hour. Just two servants were in the dining room, the wine butler and the groom of the chambers, and two footmen attending the doors. The rest of us were rushing about the kitchens and pantries trying to help Mr. Spedding find the grapes. This was a catastrophe! Mr. Spedding took his job so seriously and did everything so perfectly, that to have something go wrong at this important function was a reflection on his honor.

Oblivious to the drama that was taking place, the guests continued to converse in the dining room until His Majesty gave the signal that he wished to leave the table. He inclined his head slightly toward his equerry and as he rose, everyone rose with him.

Like magic the doors were thrown open, and King Edward VII and the gentlemen entered the smoking room. The "magic" could be explained by the fact that four footmen had been waiting for the signal, two within the room and two outside of the doors, ready to fling them open the instant His Majesty came to his feet.

The next morning I was the lead on first duty. It was a little past ten o'clock and I was in the pantry putting away some of the breakfast dishes. As I turned around, I faced one of the Palace footmen who had entered so quietly that I had not heard him.

"What the devil are you doing here!" I said with a start, sensing a kind of stealth in his unusual entrance.

Ignoring my remark he whispered, "Are you alone, Gorst?"

"Yes."

"Where is Askew?"

"He's working in the smoking room. Why?"

"I'll show you!" he said. "Follow me!"

And with this announcement, he went to the other side of the pantry and opened the cupboard doors which enclosed the sink. And there, untouched and unspoiled, were the prize grapes! They were carefully tied to the main pipe, decorating the plumbing in a most bizarre way. Quickly the footman cut the string and put them in a valise which he had brought with him.

I was speechless with surprise and outrage. I finally managed to say, "What's the matter with you—have you gone mad? If Mr. Spedding finds out he'll have you put in jail!"

But the footman was bent on his purpose, and the determined way that he went about it made me realize that, short of a fist fight, I couldn't stop him. He looked at me angrily and said,

"You keep out of this, Gorst. This is my business. And don't go squealing about this either, or you'll answer to me."

Then without another word he went into Mr. Spedding's office to collect his gratuity which the Duke of Portland had left for the Palace footmen. He was a cool one all right! He walked out with the grapes right under Mr. Spedding's nose.

The day after the incident Mr. Spedding posted a notice of a five-pound reward for any information about the theft of the grapes, no questions asked. But for no price would I denounce a fellow servant. If a valuable piece of the gold service had been stolen, I would have felt differently, but the grapes weren't important enough to make me an informer.

Several days later, there was an occurrence in the household which required me to be an informer—but on this occasion I myself was the culprit. During breakfast, while Askew and I were busy setting up the sideboard, the little Marquess of Titchfield entered the serving pantry.

"There seems to be something wrong with my watch," he said. "Could you suggest some way to make it go?"

His request came at a most inopportune moment. I was preparing to carry several dishes into the dining room and I was preoccupied.

"I do wish there was an easy way to repair it, Gorst," he continued. "Can't you suggest anything?"

I was impatient to get on with my work, so I said, "I know a good way of getting it done quickly. Take the watch to the stillroom and have one of the maids pour hot butter in it."

"I've never heard of that," he said. "It seems like an odd way of making it go, but I'll try it if you say so."

Late that afternoon, Osborne came into the footmen's pantry looking worried and upset.

"His Grace wants the four of us in the study immediately," he announced. "He's in a towering rage, and the young Marquess is with him. It's something about a watch."

As we entered, I saw that the Duke had the watch in his hand and I knew that the works must be hopelessly clogged.

"I have asked my son which one of you advised him to pour butter into this watch," His Grace stated angrily.

Then he turned to the boy and said, "I will give you another chance to tell me who did this."

"I prefer not to say, Father," the Marquess of Titchfield replied, shifting nervously from one foot to another.

"I did it, Your Grace," I said stepping forward. "I really meant no harm when I made this perverse suggestion, except that the young Marquess came into the pantry while I was very busy. I'm sorry and I apologize. I would be glad to have the watch repaired."

"That won't be necessary," His Grace said unmollified, "but in the future let's not have any more wretched jokes played on twelve-year-old boys."

I left the Duke's study feeling sheepish and downcast and I could not forget the incident. Early the next morning, the little Marquess himself dissipated my embarrassment and self-reproach.

He walked into the pantry carrying a billiard cue. He looked up at me and smiled as he put it into my hand.

"That's for you, Gorst," he said with the disarming forgiveness of the young and innocent, "because I like you for telling my Father that you did it. I never would have given you away myself."

One of the most important servants of the Upper Ten, serving under Mr. Spedding, was the Duke's valet, Mr. Lane. He was an extremely prissy man, always arrogant and overbearing. He treated the footmen like serfs. He considered us so far down on the social scale that we were barely worthy of his notice! But one fine day I saw his dignity thoroughly ruffled.

The Duke of Portland was leaving 3 Grosvenor Square to attend His Majesty's Levée. The hall porter, Askew, and

I were in the front hall to assist at his departure. It was very hot in the early afternoon, and His Grace, as Master of the Horse, was in full uniform. He was impatient and uncomfortably warm. Suddenly the Duke noticed he did not have his cloak, and Mr. Lane dashed back to fetch it. When he returned, he leaned toward His Grace to put it over his shoulders.

After Mr. Lane had straightened the folds of the cloak, the Duke frowned in obvious displeasure.

"Confound it, Lane," he said angrily, "I would rather smell whiskey on your breath than listen to the crunching of coffee beans in my ear!"

Revenge was sweet!

Jim and I were not above pettiness and we saw to it that the entire household soon heard that Mr. Lane's habit of chewing coffee beans was no longer an effective camouflage for whiskey breath. The next day, Mr. Lane found some clove-flavored pastilles on his plate with an anonymous note reading:

"Guaranteed to kill the smell of whiskey or your money back."

At 3 Grosvenor Square, the upper servants lived in the house, and the footmen lived over the stables, which were called the mews. In medieval times the King's falcons were kept in cages in the stables while they were in molt. Their muffled cries were referred to as "the mewing of the King's hawks." So the words mews had come down to us from antiquity to describe the rows of stables (presently garages) which line many of the squares at the back of great London town houses.

A staircase from the mews led directly to the Servants' Hall in the basement where the Lower Five ate their meals. The upper servants ate in the housekeeper's room, so the two groups were as geographically and socially divided as they were at Welbeck. The hall boys slept on cots in the Servants' Hall and the poor little chaps waited on us for three meals a day. I don't think that during the week any of them ever left the basement or saw the light of day.

Our own work was hardly easy. Everything was carried from the kitchen to the dining room on enormous wooden trays placed on shelves and trestles hidden behind a beautiful black-and-gold Chinese screen. None of the service was visible to the guests seated at the table, and for the most part, they could not hear us puff as we arrived at the first floor from the basement, somewhat breathless from the effort of carrying up the food.

One evening, there was a Court Ball at Buckingham Palace and the Duke and Duchess dined alone at home. Askew was the lead and I was the follow-up, so I carried up the last course from the kitchen. I had a small tray with two plates and the savory, in this case, "angels on horseback," or oysters wrapped in bacon on skewers. As I came around the screen I slipped on the polished floor and the angels were no longer on horseback! They were lying on the carpet in full view of the Duke and Duchess of Portland.

"Well, Winnie, the oysters are dying on the floor and that's the end of the savory," His Grace said.

"Yes, my dear," she replied. "It reminds me of *Alice in Wonderland*. I'm a little sorry for all the poor oysters."

"But now we had better dress," His Grace said, smiling

at the allusion. "We must be at the Palace within the hour."

When the Duke and Duchess attended an event at Buckingham Palace, it was their privilege to use a state carriage. A Royal carriage was ordered at the Palace much in the same manner that one would today engage a special limousine. A telephone call to the King's head coachman insured immediate action.

When we arrived at the Palace, one footman would open the carriage door and the other pulled down the collapsible steps. Then we both stood with one arm extended so that the Duke and Duchess could grasp them as they stepped down onto the red carpet. The carriages were almost three feet off the ground, and a lady's train particularly required a footman's help.

Hales and I were on duty together for the Duke and Duchess but we were not on Palace duty this evening. While the ball was in progress we waited outside in the Buckingham Palace Quadrangle.

I was thirsty and hungry, so I told Hales that I wanted to get a small sandwich and a glass of champagne, and that I would be back before the ball was over. I went into the Palace through a side entrance to the corridor which led to the wine room.

Then I hurried through a bit of supper, which could not have taken more than twenty minutes, and went directly back to the Quadrangle. To my utter consternation, I learned from the linkman who was in charge of the carriages that my carriage had left without me. This was certainly my unlucky day!

I took a hackney back to Grosvenor Square because we were not allowed to appear walking anywhere in full-state liveries. When I reached home Hales told me, with great amusement, what had happened.

The Duke and Duchess of Portland suddenly appeared in the Quadrangle with Lady Charles Cavendish, who was feeling indisposed and too ill to remain at the ball. His Grace gave orders to the coachman to proceed to Lady Cavendish's residence in Grosvenor Crescent. But Hales did not hear the order—he was looking around for me, hoping that I would come out of the Palace in time.

As the carriage drove out of the Palace Gate, the coachman turned to the right to go to Grosvenor Crescent. But Hales began to shout, "Go to the left—go to the left! What's the matter with you!" The coachman, who had heard the Duke's order, just flicked his whip over the back of the carriage, ignored Hales, and drove on. Here was a semi-state carriage making its way through the London night with only one footman. A shocking state of affairs!

When they reached Lady Cavendish's residence, Hales helped her out and saw her to the door. Then His Grace said, "Home please, Hales." Hales again mounted the platform alone. When they arrived back at 3 Grosvenor Square, the Duke got out of the carriage, turned to the coachman and said:

"Please ask the footmen not to speak so loudly on the carriages. It is most annoying."

His Grace thought that Hales was shouting at me, yet he never noticed that I was absent. What a stroke of luck!

When the Duke and Duchess were not attending state functions, they used their own carriages. If they joined the fashionable "dress parade in Hyde Park," they preferred the Duchess' beautiful barouche drawn by her four magnificent greys and her "tiger" was on the box with the coachman.

The "tiger" was a small groom under five feet who was training to be a jockey. He wore a diminutive copy of the coachman's livery, even to the white wig, which gave an additional bit of dash to this eye-filling turnout. While the carriages drove back and forth, no motor cars were allowed in Hyde Park, so the horses would not be frightened. The Park was crowded with people who came to see the elegant procession and watch the carriages go by.

The barouche was a large open coach slung on balanced C-springs. It had four wheels, two double seats which faced each other, and a folding top that could be quickly lowered in case of rain. It was painted in shiny, dark blue and Her Grace's crest was enameled on the doors. Very often the Duke of Portland accompanied Her Grace, and he himself helped the Duchess into the carriage. Then he lifted up the "tiger" from the sidewalk and swung him on to the box beside the coachman. His Grace seemed to enjoy the little fellow and he always said, "Shoulders back and fold your arms!" The tiny groom straightened up like a tin soldier and rode as proudly on the box as though he were a general.

Every morning at seven, the Duke of Portland and Lady Victoria had a quick cup of tea and proceeded to Hyde Park where they rode in Rotten Row, a famous bridle path, and always with a groom in attendance. At the conclusion of their morning's canter, a carriage met them at Hyde Park Corner Gate, where there was another groom waiting to return the horses to the mews. When they re-

turned to Grosvenor Square, they enjoyed a hearty breakfast, and His Grace was always in good spirits, especially
if the weather had been pleasant.

His Grace loved horses and hated any kind of cruel
practices either in training them or in developing their
appearance. He was one of the first men in England to stop
the docking of horses' tails. It deeply offended him to see
an animal whipped by a coachman.

One evening as we were returning home, an empty
carriage passed us. The coachman was furiously whipping
the horses. His Grace gave orders for us to follow the man,
who proved to be Lord Windsor's coachman. The Duke
had him arrested for cruelty to animals but he did not press
the charges. Nevertheless, he had the coachman dismissed,
because His Grace believed that no man who would abuse
an animal deserved to have a responsible job.

While I served the Duke and Duchess of Portland, I
paid meticulous attention to the rules for the Royal service.
However, sometimes they seemed unnecessarily compli-
cated and involved. For a long time I particularly wanted
to have my photograph taken in my full-state livery. In
order to do so, I had to have permission both from the
Sergeant Footman at Buckingham Palace and the Duke of
Portland.

Somehow I never got around to it; the whole thing
seemed like too much trouble at the time. So now when I
see a color photograph of a Royal carriage with the footmen in the livery of Her Majesty, Queen Elizabeth II, I
am always a little saddened because I neglected to obtain
permission to have the picture made.

But I console myself with the thought that my mental image is as clearly and sharply in focus as any camera, and that by now the photograph that was never taken might be only a shapeless and faded blur.

16

---⌇---

Buckingham Palace

As the London season progressed, the great events naturally centered about Buckingham Palace. The Duke and Duchess of Portland attended all of the Court functions, so that we four Royal footmen were on constant duty both in the Palace and on the state carriages.

During the height of the season King Alphonso XIII of Spain came to London for a visit with Their Majesties, King Edward VII and Queen Alexandra. This was the young King's first visit to England and he was accorded a regal welcome. He had the usual parade for visiting Royalty, followed by a luncheon at the Guild Hall of London. The streets were lined with people who cheered and threw flowers in his path.

Surely this slight, young monarch, still in his early twenties, must have been thrilled at receiving so warm a reception. It was said that his boyhood had been austere and gloomy. His later life was also destined to be sad, ending in exile far from his native land. But on his triumphal reception into London, there was no hint of his unhappy future.

On the first night of King Alphonso's visit, King Edward VII and Queen Alexandra gave a banquet in his honor. One hundred and fifty guests were seated at one long table with semicircular ends. It was the first time in twenty-five years that a banquet was served in the Picture Gallery, which provided as handsome a background as human artistry could contrive.

The Crown gold was used throughout the dinner, and masses of orchids and lilies of the valley decorated the table. Gold vases in the center of the table graduated downward from a height of four feet, with gold candelabras arranged between them. Smilax were entwined in ropes on the table with orchids and lilies of the valley interlaced among them.

The underbutlers (there were ten or twelve who were technically footmen) attended to the silver and gold plate and the setting of the table. The rest of the staff of footmen served the banquet. We did not speak audibly at any time because we knew the routine perfectly. If there was an occasional whisper, it was drowned out by the string orchestra playing current tunes and light opera arias in the musicians' gallery.

The amazing fact about the banquet was its brevity. From the time that the guests were seated until the ladies withdrew, only a few minutes more than an hour had passed. The custom of having shorter dinners was instituted by Queen Victoria who found, as she grew older, that long state functions wearied and bored her.

His Majesty, King Edward VII, continued her innovation which was adopted by the Court Circle and English society. The servants, who prepared and served the dinners and banquets, were wholeheartedly in favor of this regime because it lightened the work, even though a great deal more deftness and speed were required.

During the banquet for King Alphonso, the Beafeaters, the yeomen of the Royal guard, stood at intervals around the gallery. They were dressed in their medieval costumes with round, stiff hats and they stood at attention with javelins in their hands, rigidly posed like living statues.

I had seen many lavish dinners and sumptuous festivities, but this dinner was the most beautiful function, the most magnificent array of imperial elegance that took place in Buckingham Palace during my service. King Edward VII was in full dress uniform, Queen Alexandra wore a white satin gown with the blue ribbon of the Garter and a glittering tiara. The ladies were resplendent in gorgeous gowns, and the gentlemen wore knee breeches and all of their decorations and orders. The table was illuminated by golden candelabras bearing hundreds of candles whose light sparkled in a sea of priceless jewels. The scene represented the golden Edwardian era at its crowning height.

When the Duchess of Portland attended a Court function, she, like Her Majesty, Queen Alexandra, wore a white satin gown or the palest of ecru satin. The pearls forming her "dog collar," and others looped in ropes about her neck, were as precious and as well matched as any known string of pearls in the world. She wore a diamond tiara at the banquet for King Alphonso and long, pear-shaped diamond earrings hung down several inches from her ear lobes. Even though she was extremely tall, she was very graceful and knew how to move and walk. She had a truly aristocratic bearing, the embodiment of what one might rightly call, a noblewoman.

As the dinner was ending, a bagpiper entered the gallery and played a swirl while he walked around the enormous table three times. Immediately after the last notes faded away, the Queen's signal came and the ladies rose and prepared to curtsy to the King and Queen.

His Majesty and King Alphonso stood at one side of the doorway, and the Queen and the Duchess of Portland (Mistress of the Robes to Her Majesty) stood at the other. As the ladies left the room, they curtsied first to King Edward and his Royal guest and then to Queen Alexandra. I stood at attention near the doorway as each guest twice went through this pretty gesture.

The gentlemen remained in the gallery for about a half hour, and then the dancing began in the ballroom after Their Majesties entered. When the evening finally came to a close, and Askew and I took our places at the back of the Duke of Portland's carriage, I had a sensation of giddiness from viewing so much splendor.

The second night of King Alphonso's visit was celebrated with a gala performance of *Rigoletto* at Covent Garden Opera House. The footmen who were on the carriages in the procession were allowed to stand at the back of the opera house. It proved to be a memorable experience: Enrico Caruso sang the role of the Duke of Mantua!

The opera house was gaily decorated with festoons of real flowers, and the British and Spanish flags were draped over the Royal box. The audience included Their Majesties, the Court Circle, many Ambassadors, Peers and Peeresses. They had all been invited to the opera by Royal command.

His Majesty, King Edward VII, showed a fondness for entertaining foreign royalty all his life, but he also enjoyed being a guest as well as a host. Even while he was the Prince of Wales, he often went to the Continent, particularly to France and Germany. In Berlin, where he visited his nephew, Kaiser Wilhelm II, his interests were not always confined to affairs of state. Sometimes his attentions were directed to less formal matters.

There was one man in the German Royal household to whom Prince Edward took an immediate liking, a footman, called James Hoffner. With the Kaiser's permission Prince Edward invited him to come to England as his personal servant, and Hoffner accepted.

Jim Hoffner was six feet, six inches tall, a handsome blond chap with brains as well as good looks. He was made personal footman to Prince Edward directly upon his arrival in England, and he attended to all of the personal needs of the Prince of Wales. He brought his breakfast tray every morning when he awakened him, and waited on him, hand and foot, every hour of the day. Jim Hoffner was still at the Palace when I joined the Royal service, and I became extremely fond of him.

Whenever it was possible for him to be off duty, Hoffner would join Askew and me for an evening. We loved to hear him speak because he had never managed to rid himself of his German accent. One night we were discussing the possibility of a war with Germany.

"What would you do if fighting broke out between Germany and England?" I asked him.

"I would fight for de King!" he shouted.

"Which king?" I continued.

"For *my* king! King Edvard, *natürlich!*" he said.

Hoffner put in an appearance in the Footmen's Room several times a week, and whenever he came down he always had a story to tell us. He said that one day two Americans were standing outside of the Winter Palace in Berlin where a large crowd had gathered. One American spoke German but the other did not.

The chap who couldn't speak German turned to his friend and asked him to find out what was causing all the excitement in the streets. So he questioned a German standing near him and translated the answer for his friend: "The German said that the pigheaded Emperor is going for an airing this morning." A policeman standing nearby overheard these remarks and arrested all of them.

The fellow who spoke German said, "Why do you arrest me? What have I done?"

The policeman said, "You have insulted the Emperor!"

The American said, "You've got me wrong! I didn't mean *your* Emperor—I was talking about the Emperor of China!"

"Oh, no, you weren't," the policeman said. "You were speaking of *our* Emperor—there is only *one* pigheaded Emperor!"

The Footmen's Room in Buckingham Palace was our dressing room in addition to being a meeting place. Here each man had an individual cupboard so that he was not obliged to traverse the long distance to the Footmen's Lobby where the Palace footmen lived. Among the supply of personal accessories we kept on hand were many extra pairs of spotlessly clean white cotton gloves (which we were required to wear at all times) and all of our powdering equipment.

Next to the Footmen's Room was the Powder Room, where we fixed our hair and put on our liveries. It was a rule that all powdering was to be done only in the Powder Room to keep the penetrating dust out of the footmen's rooms in the Palace.

There was also a Boot Room in the Palace basement where all uniforms were wet-brushed and shoes were cleaned. This was done when the footmen were off duty and each man was responsible for keeping his liveries in perfect order—everything of course done under the watchful eyes of Mr. Hawkins.

Mr. Hawkins, the Sergeant Footman, gave out all of our daily assignments when we were on Palace duty. So it was absolutely necessary to consult the roster which listed the liveries to be worn, the carriages to which we were assigned, and exactly where we were posted during a Palace event. When we were in Buckingham Palace, we had to wear an "off duty" livery even when we were not serving. This consisted of a black full-dress suit, black Wellington boots, a white dress shirt, round collar and a white bow tie.

There were four "indoor" liveries: the "off duty" livery; the "on duty" livery for luncheon and dinner, which was the small, scarlet coat; the formal luncheon and dinner livery, which was also a scarlet coat but trimmed with gold epaulets; and the full-state livery for important functions. This was the royal-blue Quaker coat worn with purple knee breeches, pink silk stockings, black pumps with gold buckles, and powdered hair.

When we were on the carriages, there were also four liveries which might be ordered: postillion livery, which might require an "epaulet" or "small scarlet" coat with buckskin breeches, depending on the importance of the event; a semi-state carriage livery worn with a three-caped scarlet coat and a Napoleon hat decorated with a crest. The full-state carriage livery was the same as the semi-state livery except that we wore a pink feather on the crest of the Napoleon hat, a gilt sword, and carried a long, gold-headed stick from which hung a gold tassel.

All of these liveries were the choice of Queen Victoria. His Majesty, King Edward VII, had elected to continue them although each king had the right to select the liveries of his servants. Only the buttons had been altered to "E R VII" and they bore his crest. Being a Royal footman meant a great many dressings and undressings during the week, and the Footmen's Room was in constant use.

On one occasion while I was on Palace duty, Her Majesty, Queen Alexandra, actually spoke to me. I was walking through the Royal Corridor past the Royal Apartment, when Her Majesty stepped into the corridor.

"May I ask your name?" she said.

"Gorst, Your Majesty," I replied.

"Gorst, would you kindly go and tell Miss Knox, my secretary, that I would like to see her in my sitting room immediately?"

I bowed and said, "Yes, Your Majesty."

I fetched that secretary with as much dispatch and conscientiousness as though I had been commanded to establish an outpost of the empire!

In one of the remote corners of Buckingham Palace, a

small workshop had been built. Here Franz, a young Austrian, whom His Majesty had brought to England from Vienna, made exquisite forms and sculptures of spun sugar.

Of all the lovely things he created, I thought his masterpieces were the life-size swans with hollowed-out backs in which petits fours and cakes could be served. His Majesty, just like the rest of us, often came to Franz' little *atelier* to watch him work.

Franz received a large salary for his work and he deserved it. His creations added immeasureably to every Palace function where they were used, and many of the distinguished guests congratulated and complimented the Master of the Household.

One day Mr. Hawkins gave me a small basket Franz had made, and I tried to pack it ever so carefully to send to my sister, Lily. It was made entirely of roses molded of sugar paste, and the leaves and stems, fashioned of crystallized sugar, had the delicacy of spun glass. Even though I encased it in cotton floss, I decided it would never reach her without being damaged, so I kept it for her in my room in the mews.

The Garden Party, given toward the end of June each season at Buckingham Palace, was one of the most picturesque and charming events on the Palace calendar. The refreshments were served under a large marquee on the lawn. The ladies wore attractive gowns with lacy frills and furbelows, and large garden hats trimmed with maline and artificial flowers. Undoubtedly each dress had been specially ordered for the occasion, because the lovely ladies seemed so self-assured and aware that they were displaying the latest fashion. There were about two thousand guests who moved slowly about, chatting and visiting with each other. The scene was like a painting of a summer landscape with elegant figures strolling on the lawns, promenading through the gardens of flowers and shrubs in full bloom.

We, who served at the Garden Party, enjoyed it more than any other event during the London season. The service was simple and required little effort. It was easy to pour the tea and champagne, and the footmen passed small sandwiches, so we were able to look on and enjoy the relaxed and informal atmosphere.

There were many garden parties during the London season. One of the largest was given by the American Ambassador, Mr. Whitelaw Reid, and Mrs. Reid. This gracious lady was extremely popular in London. Their Majesties, King Edward VII and Queen Alexandra, together with their suite, and the Duke and Duchess of Portland, attended the party which was given at Dorchester House, then the American Embassy.

A memorable conversation took place that afternoon. His Majesty met Mrs. Reid's father, Mr. Darius Ogden Mills, and in the course of their friendly talk, His Majesty extended an invitation to Mr. Mills to attend his next Levée.

Mr. Mills scowled, looked at the King, and then very deliberately said, "A fine sight I would be in knee breeches, Your Majesty! If you will pardon me, I would rather not attend!"

His Majesty was most amused and offered a gracious compromise.

"Mr. Mills," he said, "if you promise to come, I will command long trousers to be worn."

So Mr. Mills went to the King's Levée in long trousers and he continued to receive exceptional favor from His Majesty. Mr. Mills never seemed at a loss under any circumstances, and he never sacrificed his own sincerity nor kowtowed to anyone. He spoke with the King just as he did with anyone else, and it was his brusque, American honesty which His Majesty found so disarming.

His Majesty's Levées were held at St. James' Palace in the early afternoon, and this was a reception, or presentation, for gentlemen only. Everyone appeared in his official uniform. Most of the gentlemen usually wore knee breeches, black silk stockings and pumps, but all officers were required to wear full-dress uniforms. Among the guests were foreign Ambassadors and dignitaries, and it was a great honor for visiting notables to be presented at Court.

The presentation for ladies was an evening function, known as a Drawing Room. There were three or four during the year, and usually one fell during the London season.

When the young debutante came to the Palace to be presented at Court, she arrived in her own carriage accompanied by her mother, or a chaperone. The carriages entered the gate, under the first arch, and drove to the main entrance in the Palace Quadrangle where the linkman stood ready to open the carriage doors.

Alighting from the carriages, they went into the Palace Hall where six footmen received them and led them up the great staircase to the second floor cloak rooms.

There the ladies disposed of their wraps and added the last tremulous, finishing touches to their toilettes. When they were ready, the second floor footmen showed them to one of the five drawing rooms. Here they were met by their sponsors, or the Ambassador's wife, who was introducing them. And here they awaited their turn to be taken into the Throne Room.

Then the King and Queen's personal equerry took charge of the presentation card. He gave it to the Palace Comptroller who announced them to Their Majesties. This announcement was whispered, not called out as was customary at Court Balls.

In the meantime, Their Majesties entered the ballroom with a roll of drums, followed by the playing of the National Anthem. King Edward VII escorted the lovely Queen at the head of the Royal procession. Their Majesties were preceded by the Lord Chamberlain and the Lord Steward, who walked into the ballroom backwards, holding their staves of office before them. They turned away simultaneously, as though they were executing a well-rehearsed dance, in order to allow the Royal procession to pass, because no one was permitted to turn his back on Their Majesties. This was a difficult maneuver—to back up in a straight line took years of practice—and they executed it with consummate skill.

When each of the debutantes was presented, she curtsied first to His Majesty and then to Queen Alexandra, and kissed her hand. When a young lady is nervous, a curtsy takes its toll of shaking knees, but most of them were able, after weeks of coaching and curtsying before their own mirrors, to incline themselves slightly forward, bend their knees gracefully, and then back away from the Throne. After that the young lady was led to her seat in the ballroom by two footmen, who were called the King's footman and the Queen's footman.

When all of the debutantes were finally presented, they were shown through the corridor to the Household Dining Room where a supper was laid on buffet tables. The tables went halfway around the room, close to the walls, with just enough space allowed for serving. On the opposite side of the room, long tables were set up just as they were at a Court ball, at waist height. The guests stood and ate at this level because it was difficult to sit down without mussing and crushing their beautiful gowns.

There were many footmen and pages at the back of the buffet tables who served the repast, which started with bouillon, followed by all kinds of cold entrées of birds (game and chicken), cold ham, small sandwiches of all kinds, and concluded with ices, petits fours in ornamental baskets, and cakes. Champagne was served throughout the meal. But the young ladies ate practically nothing—they were much too excited!

At supper the fathers, brothers, and gentlemen friends joined the debutantes, and they did justice to the buffet. We were kept very busy serving champagne, always the most popular beverage at a Drawing Room supper. Their Majesties did not join the large assemblage in the Household Dining Room. They had their supper served in the Royal Dining Room with a few friends in attendance.

I enjoyed the presentation ceremonies because I loved to look at the young ladies whose youthful complexions were glowing and heightened by the supreme moment which they were experiencing. Even the plainest of them seemed to become beautiful, illuminated by some hidden, inner radiance and expectation.

We were instructed to address everyone as "M'am" and "Sir," regardless of rank. Theoretically, this seemed to me to be inadequate—surely so many lovely, young creatures deserved to be addressed more imaginatively even by a Palace footman!

However, in practice, this order did not work out well for me. I was standing behind the waist-high buffet table ready to serve the guests. A lady in an extremely elaborate gown approached the table and said in the unmistakable accent of an American Southerner:

"I want an ice"—pronouncing it "ay-ess."

"Pardon me M'am," I replied, "the ices are served in the Green Drawing Room."

"I want an ice served to me—right here!" she said glaring at me.

"I'm sorry, *Madam*," I said unthinkingly, "we cannot serve the ices here. Perhaps you would like a glass of champagne?"

"I don't want any champagne," she said angrily. "Will you get me an ice or won't you?"

"No, Madam, I cannot leave the buffet," I said.

"Who is in charge here?" she demanded.

At that moment the Comptroller heard the disturbance and joined us.

"This footman has been terribly rude to me," she complained. "He will not serve me an ice."

"Were you rude to this lady, Gorst?" the Comptroller asked quietly.

"No, my lord, I don't believe I was. I am not permitted to go to the Green Room to serve an ice nor leave my station."

"Perhaps you'd better leave the room for a bit," he said as he winked at me.

As I turned to leave, I saw him offer his arm to the lady, which she accepted with a slight curtsy.

"I will personally escort you to the Green Drawing Room and see that you have an ice," he said tactfully. By this time, the lady had forgotten all about me, she was so flattered at having such a distinguished escort.

But the Comptroller did not forget me. A few moments later, he stood in the doorway and smiled at me. He clapped his hands in silent applause and nodded his head approvingly.

After the supper had been served and the guests were ready to leave, the footmen who were to go on the carriages were given a signal by the Sergeant Footman to get ready.

I hurried down to the Palace entrance and found that Hales was already on the carriage, so I waited near the door to be on hand when the Duke and Duchess of Portland appeared on the steps.

A distinguished-looking gentleman walked up to me and looked me over from top to toe.

I heard him mutter to himself, "By Gad! The British dress their footmen a damned sight better than they do their diplomats!"

I asked the Palace linkman who the speaker was, and I discovered that I had been appraised by Lord Strathcona, High Commissioner for Canada. At that moment I saw the Duke and Duchess of Portland on the stairs, and I ran into the Quadrangle to get on the carriage in order to be ready when the linkman called.

The instant the linkman signaled to us, we drove up to the entrance and helped Her Grace and the Duke into a semi-state carriage, a closed and spacious conveyance.

That evening His Grace seemed grateful for the comfortable, tufted upholstery. He fell fast asleep during the drive home.

When we helped Her Grace alight, she turned to Hales and me and said:

"I hope you don't mind my saying so—but both of you look rather drawn. Are you feeling well?"

"I can speak for myself," Hales replied. "I'm perfectly well, Your Grace, but this has been the most hectic season I have ever known!"

"And you, Gorst?" she inquired.

"I'm as well as Hales, Your Grace," I said smiling at her. "But if I may say so, I agree with him about the season."

"Yes, I understand," she said sympathetically. "I know the hours have been long. But soon we will be going to Scotland and then things will be much quieter and simpler for you." After that she said good night to us in her inimitable, gracious way.

17

Langwell in County Caithness

WHEN the Portland household went from London to Scotland, to the Duke and Duchess of Portland's estate, Langwell, in County Caithness, it was like moving a small army. It required a special train to transport us to Helmsdale on the North Sea. We referred to it as the "iron caravan."

The Duke and Duchess occupied one car, which was comparable to a "private car" in America, consisting of several bedrooms, a sitting room, and a dining area; the children and the governess occupied the next car; the Upper Ten rode next; then the footmen, the chef and his helpers, and chauffeurs; and the final passenger car was reserved for stillroom maids and housemaids. The rest of the train was a long string of box cars, each one housing an automobile.

Every time we stopped, Hales went forward to see if Her Grace wished anything, although she had her own personal maid. Hales was the only one in uniform, wearing

the small scarlet coat and black trousers of a Royal traveling footman. But it didn't bother him in the least to be the
only one who wasn't wearing mufti, he was so intensely
proud of his job.

The railroad served the Duke's and Duchess's meals. All
the servants had tea baskets with sandwiches, chicken, hard-
boiled eggs, and fruit which had been packed before we
left London. It really was one, big picnic! Two of us
shared a hamper, containing an alcohol stove and a teapot,
so that we could make our own tea. We were responsible
for the wicker hampers, which were fitted with plates and
utensils. Anyone who lost his hamper didn't eat until we
got to Scotland fourteen hours later.

Askew and I had volunteered to share our compartment
with two beautiful collies who were going to Langwell.
Whenever the train stopped for a few minutes, we took
them for a short run and an airing along the tracks. When
we stopped at Newcastle, a man opened the door of our
compartment intending to get on.

"This is a private train, sir," I said.

"Humph, is that so!" he said. And as he descended the
steps, he turned around and added, "By the looks of it, it
seems rather more like a public menagerie!"

Early the next morning, when we arrived in Helmsdale,
we got off the train and the servants went to the inn for
breakfast while the motor vehicles were being unloaded
from the box cars. We were served with Loch Fyne herring
which were supposed to be the ultimate in Scottish herring
filets. They were broiled and perfectly cooked.

I had just started mine when the order came to leave
because the motor cars had arrived and were waiting to

take everyone to the house. I was so disappointed not to be able to finish my herring that I wrapped it in a clean linen handkerchief and took it into the car. The footmen were placed in a convertible lorry, a truck for either baggage or passengers, with seats along the side. As we started off, I took my herring out of my pocket, and started to eat it.

"What in blazes are you doing?" Hales asked in amazement.

"I'm finishing my breakfast, if it's all the same to you. Who knows if I'll ever eat a Loch Fyne herring again."

When the shooting season opened at Langwell, the house guests began to arrive. The gentlemen stalked stag, and went out after grouse and partridge. The Duke of Portland was just as devoted to this sport as some of his guests, yet His Grace spent a good deal of time on his golf course, which was wonderfully laid out and full of difficult sand traps. The Duchess played occasionally, but as a rule the ladies did not join the gentlemen until luncheon at Braemore, the shooting lodge.

The exception to the rule was Lady Algernon Gordon-Lenox. Lady Algy, as she was called, was a great shot. Lord Gordon-Lenox was also an enthusiast, and they vied with each other to see who could bag more game. She always accompanied the gentlemen and enjoyed shooting so much that she stayed at Braemore overnight rather than miss the early-morning start. Usually there were three servants, a cook, one footman (Osborn), and a housemaid at the lodge. They all rose at dawn to serve breakfast and attend Lady Algy and the gentlemen.

When the gentlemen went out in the morning, they wore tweed jackets, knickerbockers, heavy boots, and thick wool socks which turned down over the knickerbockers at the knee. Some wore sport caps, and others wore old fedoras, with a cockade of grouse feathers or a marksmanship badge stuck in the band.

When the ladies joined the gentlemen at luncheon, they had on tweed suits with skirts that came just below the knees, in contrast to the skirts they usually wore that came down to their high-buttoned shoes. It was already becoming fashionable to dress for comfort and for informality. It would have been absurd to walk in long, uncomfortable skirts in Scotland where everything, by its very nature, demanded simplicity.

Langwell stood on the cliffs overlooking the North Sea. It was an imposing stone mansion that boasted none of the splendor of Welbeck, but its spacious rooms afforded the greatest comfort. The Duke and Duchess occupied a suite of four rooms, and there were two commodious guest suites in the wings. The grounds were dotted with houses and cottages. The children and the governess lived in one, and the Upper Ten had their own; there were several houses kept in readiness for guests, and the cottages were assigned to the servants in groups.

We four footmen shared our quarters with the nursery footman and the schoolroom footman. All the maids lived in one cottage, which was again politely dubbed the "Virgins' Wing."

The estate looked like a lovely small village with the streets and graveled walks intertwined among the white houses and quaint cottages. The landscape was barren and stern and only the grounds near the house were planted with lawns, flower beds, and shrubs. There were no extensive gardens; Scaraben and Morven contributed their own rugged mountain beauty!

At Langwell, the footmen were allowed to use the golf course, swim, and go salmon fishing. When we fished for salmon, we were allowed to catch only one a day, and it had to be inspected by a gillie who took good care that no fish was caught illegally. The Duke of Portland had given orders that all salmon were to be taken from the river with flies, and any infringement of this order was to be reported to him.

One Sunday afternoon, the Duke and Duchess and their guests had gone to Dunrobin Castle on the North Sea to spend the day with the Duke and Duchess of Sutherland. Jim and I were free. We went to the river laden with equipment to catch our allowance of salmon. While I was getting the gear ready, I noticed Jim lying on a flat rock projecting out over the stream.

"Fred," he called, "have you ever seen anybody 'tittle' a salmon?"

"No, Jim," I replied. "I don't know what you're talking about!"

"Well, come over here and I'll show you something rather odd."

I walked over to the jutting rock where Jim was lying, and as he cautioned me to be silent, I looked down into the stream where a large salmon was lying almost motionless just below the surface of the water.

"Is he asleep?" I whispered.

"I don't know," Jim said. "But watch carefully."

Jim put his hand and arm gently into the water and very slowly ran his fingers under the salmon's belly. The fish seemed to stiffen, and with this amazing reflex, even the fins appeared to stop moving. Jim grabbed the fish with both hands and pulled it quickly out of the water.

"There you are, Fred!" he cried triumphantly.

"That's quite a good trick," I admitted, "but you'd better not let the gillies see this salmon—it wasn't caught with a fly!"

"I'll fix that," Jim said. And he ripped the salmon's mouth with a hook so that it would appear to have been caught legally.

He explained that "tittling" was an old poacher's trick, and though there were other illicit methods of trapping salmon, this was the best. However it wasn't always easy to find a twelve pound salmon taking his afternoon nap!

The gillies reported to His Grace that Askew and I had caught a fine salmon and he asked to see it. He thought it was a good catch and he complimented Askew on his prowess as a fisherman. When the Duke suggested that Askew might like to have the gillies send the fish to his family or friends at home, Askew looked so ashamed that for a moment I thought he was going to confess.

"Your Grace," he managed to say, "I would like to have the fish cooked and served to all the servants, and thank you for your kindness."

His request was granted, and the salmon was made into a delicious dish called "kedjerrie." This was a mixture of salmon, diced carrots, rice, and butter moistened just enough to hold it together. In Scotland, it was served on the hot plate for breakfast but the servants could not always have it because the allowance of salmon was so limited. So Jim did give us all a treat, and I think this fact eased any lingering pangs of guilt he might have felt.

Jim and I spent much of our free time together. One pleasant morning we went for a walk along the seashore, and the water looked so inviting that we thought we would go in for a quick dip. We had no bathing suits with us but that didn't stop us. We took off our clothes and rushed into the icy waters. When we returned to the rocks to dress, we were greeted by a woman's scream. The Duchess' maid and Mr. Lane stood before us on the path!

"Go ahead and dress yourselves—we'll turn our backs on you!" Mr. Lane said. "And I'll wait. I have something to say to you."

When we were presentable, we faced Mr. Lane. We would have liked to have ducked him into the sea, but there was a lady present—and she was his latest romantic interest. And one other important fact: he was the Duke's valet and one of the Upper Ten.

"I'm going to report this to His Grace," he said, scowling at us.

"You will do *no* such thing," the maid said. "We didn't have to stay and watch them!"

"Mr. Lane," I said, "do what you like about it. And you know where you can go!"

The next day a notice was posted in the footmen's pantry, which was in the form of an order from the Duke to Mr. Spedding, that all servants must wear proper *bathing suits* when swimming! It suggested a suit with sleeves that covered the person from the shoulders to the knees. The order was signed by Mr. Spedding. Jim, outraged by the whole incident, added Mr. Lane's name under Mr.

Spedding's signature, and wrote beside it in bold letters, "THE INFORMER."

Mr. Lane took great exception to the signature which Jim had added to the bulletin, and there was quite a scene in Mr. Spedding's office. Naturally we knew that Mr. Lane had informed on us in order to make himself important in his lady-fair's eyes. Mr. Spedding finally told us to forget the matter, and emphasized that he had given orders that no personal grievance was to be taken up with His Grace, that all differences among the staff were to be settled among ourselves, and that he alone would arbitrate all disputes and misunderstandings.

We four footmen had helped Mr. Lane with the Duke's uniforms, with the cleaning of boots and shoes, or by bringing up a tray. But now all of us were much too busy to help him. I had no use for Mr. Lane after this petty incident but it served a purpose. I knew how right I had been not to inform on the Palace footman when he stole the grapes at the King's Dinner. I would have been in a class with Mr. Lane, a Judas among my fellow servants.

Nevertheless, the affair irked and frustrated me. It demonstrated how an arrogant upper servant could malign his inferiors who had neither redress nor defense. This highhanded treatment of a lower servant was part and parcel of the system that was inculcated in all of us. There were greater snobs among the servants than the nobility because we had more to lose.

If I had gone to Mr. Spedding and asked him to sack Mr. Lane, he would have reminded me that I belonged to the Lower Five, that I could not censure Mr. Lane because he was my superior and therefore untouchable. He would have undoubtedly told me to remember "my place" and pipe down.

Only Mr. Spedding could lodge a complaint against one of the Upper Ten—and from my point of view—this was the ultimate in snobbery! Episodes like this, of course, did not occur every day. Ordinarily things went smoothly, and I was soon too busy to think about the incident because more guests had just arrived.

That autumn in Scotland was memorable for many reasons. Compared to Welbeck the household functioned very informally, and the beautiful weather allowed the gentlemen to shoot every day, and the ladies were able to go for walks and drives. Even dinner, for which, of course, everyone dressed, had a more leisurely atmosphere than either at the London house or Welbeck. We had the feeling that there was abundant time to perform our duties.

But these easygoing days were coming to an end. We were once more busy from morning until night helping to close Langwell, until the next shooting season. A few house-maids remained to keep things in order, several grooms were left to care for the horses, the cottages stood with their shutters closed, and the head gillie was again in charge when the family left in October to return once more to Welbeck.

Welbeck was ready for us to walk into—it was as though we had never gone away. There was always a large permanent staff in residence and when we came back to this great house, everything was just as we had left it; even the servants' quarters were in perfect order and our beds were made! We went to the footmen's pantry to get our assignments, and from that moment on, we took up our duties as though there had never been an interruption.

I had been back at Welbeck for a week when I received a telegram from my brother, William, reading: "Please come at once. Lily is gravely ill." It was nine-thirty at night and I was on first duty, wearing breeches and powder. Mr. Spedding was not available, so I had to contact the underbutler to get permission to leave.

Mr. Owens spoke to the Duchess immediately, and Her Grace gave orders for the fastest car in the garage to take me to Worksop Station. I dressed and packed a small bag, and I was driven through the tunnel to make the ten-twenty train to Sheffield where I would change for Liverpool.

When I reached Sheffield, I learned, to my horror, that I would have to wait for two hours to make my connection. I paced up and down the platform feeling heartsick because I knew that if William had sent for me, my sister must be dying. She and John Ridley were going to be married at Christmas time. And they were planning to have a house of their own. Now it might never be.

And I regretted that I, myself, had taken things too much for granted. It was true that I had not been given a holiday in over two years, but somehow I should have found time to visit her. How neglectful I had been! All I could think of was the fragile basket of spun sugar roses that Franz had made, and how I had never sent it because I knew that it would have arrived broken. . . .

When I reached Liverpool my worst fears were realized. Lily had passed away. She had been ill for two days, and by the time her illness was diagnosed as appendicitis and an operation performed, she had developed peritonitis. After the operation she had never regained consciousness.

I met John for the first time at Lily's funeral. He knew that Lily and I were devoted to each other and I seemed to bring some solace to him. I felt that I could best make things up to Lily by being useful to him, so I arranged to remain in Liverpool for a fortnight. My job for the moment seemed relatively unimportant, and I spent the next two weeks trying to be a constant companion to John and my father.

I was struck by the simplicity and genuineness of John's character and I had ample opportunity to discover his homely virtues while he was staying at William's house. My brother and his wife, Kate, lived very unpretentiously and charmingly in their own home. With them I felt free to be myself.

There were no pressures to make me conform to the prepossessions and timidities of others, and for the first time I was rid of the rigid rules and conventions with which I had lived for so long.

Lily's death unsettled me completely, and it made me try to think about the future and what I should do with my life. I felt uneasy and perplexed. I spent part of each day walking by myself along the Mersey River because I wanted to resolve my troubled thoughts and uncertainties.

One afternoon as I sat looking out over the slate-gray waters to the horizon, I remembered how Lily and Mama had come to see me off when I sailed on the "Germanic" for America. I had promised them that I would never stay there and that I would always return to England. Now that both of them had passed away, I was free to break my pledge if I wished. And beyond the horizon, which did not seem so very far away, was America!

This restless notion, which grew out of my sadness, began to take shape and meaning. Perhaps it was time to cut the old ties, to change the scene, to seek new adventures and different vistas. And I began to realize that I wanted new experiences, despite the magnificence and glitter of the world in which I lived. Like many other young men of my age, I wanted to make a new life. Some had gone to India and Australia, but that was not my choice. I would go to America, as my father and grandfather had gone before me.

As I walked back toward the city, I wondered what I would do in America. How would I find a job—and how would I manage to live? Then I thought of Miss Massey and I decided to go to see her at once.

I told her of my decision, said that she was the first to know of my plans, and added that as always I needed her help.

"I think I understand," she said sympathetically. "And with your usual luck, you have again walked in here at exactly the right moment! Actually, Fred, I thought of you but I didn't let you know of this position because I did not think you would be interested.

"But your wish to go to America changes all that and you are completely qualified for a job which has come to the London office. It is an offer from an American gentleman, Mr. Perry Belmont, for a first footman-valet who will return to America with him. I will send them a telegram immediately and I know the job is yours if you want it. I will ring you up in the morning."

Bright and early the next day, Miss Massey called to say that Mr. Belmont had engaged me. He was leaving London in a fortnight to go to Paris, and since I would be expected to remain at Welbeck for a full month after giving notice, I would have to meet him on the Continent. This news absolutely delighted me and I blurted it out to my family. To my surprise they received my announcement very calmly.

"I have been watching you," William said with a knowing smile. "And I could have given you odds that you were off on a new tack."

Even my father was pleased, and I was happy that the whole family seemed to approve. I left that afternoon to return to Welbeck.

All of my friends were very kind to me when I returned to my duties, and their genial greetings—"Hello, old chap" and "Nice to see you back," and even "Sorry to hear about your trouble"—all of it was from the heart. This made it harder for me to go to Mr. Spedding's office to resign from my job.

But it was Askew with whom I wanted to talk most of all. He seemed stunned when I told him that I had decided to leave and that my plans were already made. I told him how much his help had meant to me over the years, and that I regretted more than anything else that we wouldn't be working together anymore. I strongly urged him to go to America with me.

But after he had thought about it, he decided to wait for a Palace vacancy and to keep his place as third in seniority of the four Royal footmen.

The day before I left for London, and my first trip to

Paris, several memorable things happened. I received a telegram from Mr. Perry Belmont.

"Meet me Ritz Hotel, Paris. Sailing on 'Kron Prinz Wilhelm' December 18 for New York."

I was overjoyed—I would have ten whole days in Paris!

Then Mr. Spedding called me to his office and wished me good luck as he presented me with an envelope containing a gift of ten pounds from the Duke and Duchess of Portland. He said that he had excused Osborn, Hales, Askew, and me from our evening duty, because he knew they were going to give me a farewell party. Mr. Spedding then shook hands with me and said:

"Gorst, if you ever get to Boston, look up my cousin, Will. He's young and adventuresome too!"

My friends had planned a good dinner, and we drank our farewell toasts over and over again. The Worksop Inn resounded to "For He's a Jolly Good Fellow," and as the time came to close the inn, we drank the last toast to Their Majesties, King Edward VII and Queen Alexandra.

We drove back to Welbeck through the Lady Bolsover Drive, and long past midnight, as we climbed the great staircase to the fifth floor, I knew that Askew and I were going back to our room together for the last time. Though it was only a few hours until my train would leave and many things were on my mind, I made no attempt at conversation. Askew, tired from a long day, lost no time in getting into bed, and soon he was peacefully asleep.

I finished a few odds and ends of packing, polished my shoes, and laid out the suit I would wear to London. Then after a final check, I put out the lights, and in the darkness I drew a chair over to the open window.

As I looked out over the expanse of the lawns glistening with frost, I thought of the swans gliding over the lake in summer, I thought of the Duchess of Portland serving tea to her guests on the magnificent East Terrace. I thought of many things: of the stately processions of Kings and Queens in which I had ridden, the call of the Palace link-man in the Quadrangle, the click of Wellington boots, and —I suppose, in a way, the symbol of it all—the changing of the Guard at Buckingham Palace!

And now on the eve of my departure I realized how difficult it would be to leave all this. It had been my life and my work for so many years. But the die was cast! There could be no change, no turning back.

A clock tolled the hour somewhere far away, a bird chattered from a distant hedgerow, and soon the darkness was touched by the first, faint streaks of another day. Suddenly, as I heard the gathering sounds of morning, my sadness turned to quiet joy.

For I realized that, although I was going to the New World, part of me would always remain here, in this beautiful land which I loved so well. But my memories and my loyalties would go with me wherever I went. They would endure and they would serve me always, as a guiding beacon lights the way for a traveler on a long, uncertain journey.